THE WORST-CASE SCENARIO
ALMANAC
HISTORY

The
WORST-CASE SCENARIO
ALMANAC
HISTORY

By Joshua Piven, David Borgenicht,
Piers Marchant, and Melissa Wagner

Illustrations by Brenda Brown

CHRONICLE BOOKS
SAN FRANCISCO

Worst-Case Scenario® and The Worst-Case Scenario Survival
Handbook™ are trademarks of Quirk Productions, Inc.

Cover image used with permission of Replogle Globes,
Broadview, Illinois.

Library of Congress Cataloging-in-Publication Data available.
ISBN-10: 0-8118-4540-0
ISBN-13: 978-0-8118-4540-3

Manufactured in Canada
Typeset in Adobe Caslon, Bundesbahn Pi, Futura, and Zapf Dingbats
Designed by Bob O'Mara
Illustrations by Brenda Brown

Visit www.worstcasescenarios.com

Distributed in Canada by Raincoast Books
9050 Shaughnessy Street
Vancouver, British Columbia V6P 6E5

10 9 8 7 6 5 4 3 2 1

Chronicle Books LLC
85 Second Street
San Francisco, California 94105
www.chroniclebooks.com

WARNING

When a life is imperiled or a dire situation is at
hand, safe alternatives may not exist. To deal with the
worst-case scenarios presented in this book, we highly
recommend—insist, actually—that the best course of
action is to consult a professionally trained expert. But
because highly trained professionals may not always
be available when the safety or sanity of individuals is
at risk, we have asked experts on various subjects to
describe the techniques they might employ in these
emergency situations. THE PUBLISHER, AUTHORS,
AND EXPERTS DISCLAIM ANY LIABILITY from
any injury that may result from the use, proper or
improper, of the information contained in this book.
We do not guarantee that the information contained
herein is complete, safe, or accurate, nor that it was
effective at the time in history when it was used.
Nothing in this book should be considered a substitute
for your good judgment or common sense, nor should
anything be construed or interpreted to infringe
on the rights of other persons or to violate criminal
statutes. We urge you to obey all laws and respect
all rights of others, especially historians.

—The Authors

CONTENTS

Those who cannot learn from history are doomed to repeat it.
—George Santayana

We learn from history that we do not learn from history.
—Georg Wilhelm Friedrich Hegel

INTRODUCTION

"History is just one damned thing after another," Winston Churchill stated succinctly, and he knew history. Other historians, philosophers, politicians, and pundits have also warned that unless we learn from the past, we are doomed to repeat it—which is just another way of admitting that the past was pretty awful and giving us the responsibility for doing something about it.

That's where *The Worst-Case Scenario Almanac: History* comes in. The only way to be truly prepared for what you might have to deal with in the future is to be prepared for what people had to deal with in the past. And who can better prepare you for the past than the authors and experts who have brought you the Worst-Case Scenario series?

The dangers of the past are considerably greater than the risks of today: What can happen to you in the next 24 hours barely registers on the scales of history when weighed against all the truly terrible things that have happened over the last five thousand or millions of years. If we are really going to learn from the disasters of history so we can avoid having to deal with them all over again, we must be ready to meet the worst events of the past head-on.

Starting with the Big Bang and ending with the year 2000, this informative and useful volume gives you 300 pages of the worst moments and critical mistakes that have made history "no more than

a tableau of crimes and misfortunes" (Voltaire).
The how-to scenarios, in the tradition of our earlier
books in the Worst-Case series, offer step-by-step
instructions on life-threatening situations, including
winning a joust, escaping from the Tower of London,
circling the wagons, and surviving when your ship
hits an iceberg.

Our dynamic new almanac format allows us to go
further and provide additional essential information:
timelines that put history in a new perspective;
Who's Who of the Worst profiles that offer fresh
insights into the villains of yesteryear; charts, dia-
grams, and lists that give new meaning to both the
technical and the trivial; and short narratives that
illuminate some of the bad decisions and turning
points of history. And we call your attention to
brief but important history lessons with Nota Bene
("mark well") entries.

With this book in hand, you will be in a much
better position to learn from history and to meet
all of life's challenges, then and now. Because when
it comes to the past, you just never know . . .

—The Authors

CAVING IN

THE ANCIENT WORLD

13–14 billion BC	Universe created in giant explosion
65 million BC	Sun obscured by dust from impact of asteroid on Yucatan Peninsula, kills off dinosaurs
3.5 million BC	Lucy, world's first known hominid, dies
1.8 million BC	Beginning of Great Ice Age
1.5 million BC	Human-like species first controls fire
10,000 BC	Alcohol discovered
7000 BC	Animals domesticated, farming begins
3500 BC	Humans migrate from newly formed North African desert to Nile River Valley
3500 BC	First Egyptian mummy created
3250 BC	Wheel invented
3100 BC	First Stonehenge built
3000 BC	Wrestling becomes world's first organized sport
2566 BC	Pyramid at Cheops at Giza finished; built by 4,000 stonemasons and 100,000 laborers
2500 BC	Egyptians discover papyrus for writing
2465 BC	Great Sphinx of Giza built; called Abu al-Hawl, or "Father of Terror," by Arabs
2300 BC	Sumerian civilization—responsible for world's first cities—invaded and overtaken by Akkadians

2200 BC	City-based civilizations in Mesopotamia, Egypt, Palestine, Crete, the Greek mainland, and in the Indus Valley collapse due to massive drought
c. 1780 BC	"An eye for an eye; a tooth for a tooth" made written law in Hammurabi's Code
1628 BC	Earthquake and volcanic eruption on island of Santorini causes tsunami; destroys Minoan civilization on Crete
1590 BC	Hittites plunder Babylon
c. 1450 BC	Egyptian Book of the Dead written
1400 BC	Invention of iron production; Hittites create superior weapons and tools
1350 BC	First smallpox outbreak
1325 BC	Tutankhamun (King Tut) dies of broken leg
1200 BC	Egyptian Empire begins decline
1180 BC	Greeks conquer Troy with Trojan Horse; destroy city
1170 BC	World's first recorded labor strike in Thebes, Egypt; workers refuse to continue pyramid construction until they receive food, drink, clothing, medicine, and back pay
753 BC	Rome founded by Romulus
710 BC	Assyrians equip palace with first lock requiring a key
600 BC	Leprosy epidemics in India, China, and Egypt
581 BC	King Nebuchadnezzar II burns Jerusalem
569 BC	Nebuchadnezzar II develops mental illness, goes into the woods to live like a wild animal

HOW TO FEND OFF A SABER-TOOTHED TIGER

1 | Fight back.
Show the tiger you are not defenseless. The saber-toothed tiger typically springs on a victim in a surprise attack, inflicting a disabling injury with its teeth or claws, then waiting nearby for its prey to die of blood loss. Do not play dead.

2 | Control the tiger's head.
The cat will use its 8-inch-long canine teeth to stab, rip, or shear at your throat. Grab the tiger's head with both hands and force it away from your head and neck.

3 | Protect your abdomen.
The animal will swat at your abdomen with its sharp front claws to try to gut you. Curl into a ball to protect your abdomen with your legs, or jump far enough away to escape the tiger's reach.

4 | Look for a weapon.
Survey your immediate surroundings for a stout downed tree branch or a large rock.

5 | Strike at the tiger's head with the weapon.
The saber-toothed tiger will likely back away after your counterattack, giving you an opportunity to escape.

6 | Climb a tree.

Saber-toothed tigers are not capable climbers, so the cat will not follow you up a tree. Grab a branch at its base and use your legs to power yourself up the tree, keeping three of your limbs in contact with the tree at all times. Climb at least 6 feet from the ground to get out of the animal's leaping range.

7 | Run.

If no tree is available, sprint. While they are capable of bursts of high speed, saber-toothed tigers are not skilled runners, and they will not follow prey over long distances. Once the tiger is injured or loses interest, run away as fast and as far as you can.

grab

grab

Grab the tiger's head with both hands and keep it away from your head and throat.

Be Aware

Saber-toothed tigers stalk prey in areas where they are able to remain hidden. Pay special attention when traveling through tall grasses and between large boulders.

Now We Know

- Unlike most modern big cats, saber-toothed tigers hunted in packs and probably had a social structure much more similar to lions than present-day tigers.
- Saber-toothed tigers were a foot shorter than lions, but twice as heavy.
- Saber-toothed tigers were common in the area that is now the western United States. Thousands of their bones have been found in the La Brea tar pits in Los Angeles, California.

HUMANS CAUSE EXTINCTION OF GIANT MAMMALS

Enormous mammals—saber-toothed tigers, giant ground sloths, mastadons, and wooly mammoths—roamed the Americas during the Great Ice Age, from 1.8 million to 10,000 years ago. But as the Ice Age ended and humans arrived in North and South America, the megafauna suddenly vanished. Warmer temperatures caused the retreat of glaciers and changed the climate on the continents, disrupting the habitats and food supplies of many large animals. This likely caused a decline in their populations, but it was the nomadic, big game–hunting humans who finished them off. Animals such as the slow-moving, 5,000-pound giant ground sloth (as large as modern-day elephants) were easy targets, unable to hide or escape from human predators who could easily outrun the animal and spear it to death. In all, by 8500 BC, at least 35 types of large mammals had disappeared from North and South America.

History Lesson: Spears don't kill, people do.

HOMO SAPIENS' EVOLUTIONARY TRADE-OFFS

Gains	Losses
Larger brains	Smaller teeth
Opposable thumbs	Prehensile toes
Bipedalism	Hair-covered bodies
Improved vision	Reduced sense of smell
Complex social lives	Guilt-free existence

ICE AGE

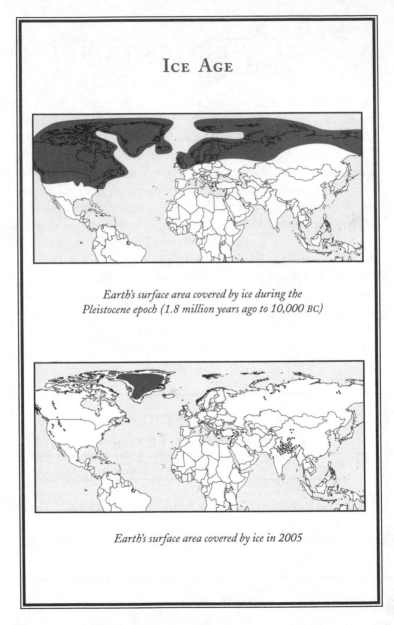

*Earth's surface area covered by ice during the
Pleistocene epoch (1.8 million years ago to 10,000 BC)*

Earth's surface area covered by ice in 2005

AKKADIANS DESTROYED BY DROUGHT

In 2200 BC, the Middle East experienced the beginning of a 300-year drought that brought the demise of several of the world's first organized societies. No civilization was more adversely affected than the Akkadians. Built by Sargon in 2334 BC, Akkad encompassed parts of present-day Syria, Iraq, and Turkey, uniting the separate city-states of the region for the first time. The Akkadians established traditions in art, literature, government, and warfare that would be mimicked for centuries to come. However, after a mere 140 years, a great drought caused the empire's collapse. The inhabitants of the northern Mesopotamian cities abandoned their homes in search of a more steady food supply when the lack of rainfall turned their fields to dust. There was a great southern migration toward fields irrigated by the Tigris and Euphrates rivers—but this area, too, was experiencing the drought. Without water, the entire Akkadian empire disappeared, its once impressive cities completely uninhabited for more than 300 years.

History Lesson: Even mighty empires are subject to Mother Nature.

WORST DISASTERS OF THE ANCIENT WORLD

Event	Year	Death Toll
Meteorite 6 miles in diameter hits Yucatan Peninsula	65 million BC	Extinction of the dinosaurs
Meteorite hits Arizona	5000 BC	Crater a mile across and 550 feet deep created upon impact
Middle Eastern drought, famine	2200 BC	Collapse of civilizations in Middle East
Santorini volcano erupts, causes tsunami	1628 BC	Wipes out Minoan Civilization
Fire of Babylon	538 BC	Destroys city, including Hanging Gardens

HOW TO DEFEND YOURSELF IN A CLUB ATTACK

1 Face your attacker(s).
Look directly at your adversary. If there are multiple attackers, rotate your body (not just your head) so that you address each foe in turn. Your body language will send a clear signal that your defense will include counterattacks aimed at each attacker.

2 Move your club into the "ready" position.
Take hold of the club securely near the bottom, an inch or two above its base. Your wrists should be firm but not locked. Position your club vertically in front of your chest, with the far end of the club angled slightly away from you. Bend your arms somewhat at the elbows.

3 Step up and into oncoming blows, pushing back with your own club.
Ignore the instinct to step away. Club blows are most dangerous when the full force of the end of the club makes contact with an object (your head). Move in close to reduce the distance the attackers' clubs can swing. Avoid extending your arms, which would make your own counterblow less powerful. To defend against hits from the side, hold your club in a vertical position, moving from side to side. To defend against blows coming from above your head or up from the ground, quickly rotate your forearms and move your club to a horizontal

wrists firm

step into
the blow

*Hold your club parallel to the ground to
defend against overhead blows.*

position, parallel with the ground. Absorb the strikes from your attackers in the middle to lower third of your club rather than at the tip, to maintain better control of your weapon and wage a more powerful defense.

4 Counterattack.
Bash, don't swing, with either end of your own club. Inexperienced club fighters may pause when their blow is successfully parried. Quickly move your club back to the ready position and strike at your opponent's head. Never raise the club up behind your head to prepare for a huge blow, as you leave your entire body vulnerable to an attack.

Be Aware
- The best clubs have a slightly gnarled "lip" at one end to prevent it from sliding out of your hands.
- Apply pine tar near the base of the club for added grip.

GREEKS TRICK TROJANS, DESTROY CITY

By 1180 BC, Greek forces had unsuccessfully besieged Troy for ten years, attempting to wrest the world's most beautiful woman, Helen, away from Paris, a Trojan prince. Greek warrior Odysseus hatched a plan, ordering the construction of a giant hollow wooden horse. When the horse was finished, several Greek soldiers, including Odysseus, climbed inside, and the horse was left outside the gates of Troy. The rest of the Greek army sailed out of sight to make it appear as though they'd abandoned the siege. The Greeks left behind one man, Sinon, who persuaded the Trojans that the horse was the retreated Greek army's offering to the goddess Athena and that the horse would provide protection to the Trojans if they took it inside the city walls. The Trojans pulled the horse into the city and celebrated their victory. Late that night, Odysseus and the soldiers climbed out of the horse through a hidden trap door. They opened Troy's gates and welcomed an awaiting Greek army, who had returned from their ships to ransack the city. The Greeks quickly overpowered the Trojans in their surprise attack and proceeded to destroy the city of Troy. Paris was killed, and Helen was returned to her Spartan husband Menelaus—though he'd intended to kill his unfaithful wife, he was soon so charmed by her beauty that he spared her. The two of them returned to Sparta to resume their life together. **History Lesson:** Always look a gift horse in the mouth.

NEBUCHADNEZZAR II
King of Babylon

BEST KNOWN FOR: Conquests of Judah and Jerusalem • Ordering death of rebel soldiers performed in front of him • Forcing rebel leader Zedekiah to watch his sons' horrible deaths, then plucking his eyes out so the last thing he would see was the misery of his family • Deporting the prominent citizens of Jerusalem • Years of madness wherein he went into the woods to behave like an animal

BORN: c. 630 BC

FAMILY: Eldest son and successor of Nabopolassar, who freed Babylon from its dependence on Assyria and laid waste to Nineveh. Nebuchadnezzar married the daughter of Cyaxares, uniting the Median and Babylonian dynasties.

FIRST JOB: Laborer in restoring the temple of Marduk, the national god of Babylonia

LEAST KNOWN FOR: Building the Hanging Gardens of Babylon, one of the Seven Wonders of the World

DEATH: 561 BC. He died of unknown causes in Babylon in the forty-third year of his reign.

HOW TO ESCAPE IF YOU ARE SEALED INSIDE A PYRAMID

1 Find the King's sarcophagus.
The sarcophagus may be unadorned and simply appear to be a large stone box or coffin. As you search, pick up useful items left behind by workers, such as additional torches, metal or stone objects that can be used as tools, and any food or drink.

2 Stand facing the sarcophagus.
The exit from the burial chamber will be on the north wall, which will be on your right. The doorway will be blocked with a huge, unmovable slab of granite.

3 Make a pick or ax.
Break some of the stone vases in the room and, using a sharp pointed section, fashion an ax by grinding it against the granite.

4 Carve around the slab.
Do not attempt to carve the slab itself. The passage surrounding the door slab is made of limestone, a rock much softer than granite. Use the ax to carve an escape hole around the slab. This is likely to take several days, so ration your food and drink accordingly.

5 Crawl through the hole to access the passageway behind the door.

Continue to follow the corridors as they slope up toward the north. Determine the proper direction by using additional granite slabs blocking the way as your guide. Carve around them as necessary.

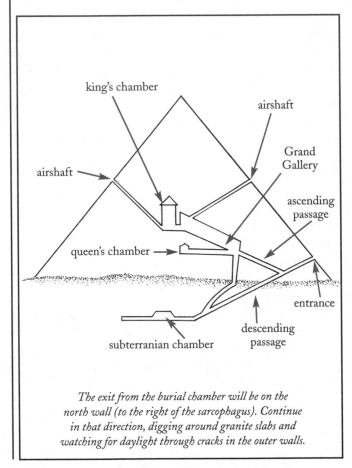

king's chamber

airshaft

Grand Gallery

airshaft

ascending passage

queen's chamber

entrance

subterranian chamber

descending passage

The exit from the burial chamber will be on the north wall (to the right of the sarcophagus). Continue in that direction, digging around granite slabs and watching for daylight through cracks in the outer walls.

6 | Feel the pyramid blocks as you make your way.
External blocks may be slightly warmer to the touch than those inside.

7 | Look for outside light.
As you approach the entrance to the pyramid, light may begin to penetrate into the darkness through cracks in the blocks.

8 | Carve around the final slab of rock.
The main entrance will be in the north face of the pyramid about 55 feet above the ground. Carve around the final slab to reach the outside, taking care not to tumble down the sloped side of the pyramid.

9 | Slide or climb down the face of the pyramid.
Flatten your body against the outer wall of the pyramid and inch your way down to the ground.

PHARAOH FACES LABOR STRIKE, PLOT ON LIFE

Ramses III, the last of the great Egyptian Pharaohs, was a skilled warrior and negotiator, having blocked three separate invasions by neighboring empires. But by 1170 BC, his fortunes changed as he faced domestic challenges on two fronts. Skilled workers at the royal necropolis near Thebes, whose wages of grain, clothing, ointment, fish, and vegetables were reduced and delayed by crooked administrators, staged the world's first recorded labor strike in demand of immediate payment. After the strike went on for several days, high-ranking officials intervened and delivered the back wages, but the display was an embarrassing sign of corruption and vulnerability in the Pharaoh's government. Soon afterwards, Tiy, one of the Pharaoh's "lesser" wives, exploited the Pharaoh's faltering popularity by hatching a plot against his life. She intended to murder Ramses with the fatal bite of a poisonous snake, with the intention of elevating her son, Pabakamon, to the throne. Tiy convinced the ladies of the harem and several of the Pharaoh's closest advisors to assist in the scheme. The plot was discovered and the conspirators were brought to trial—and though Ramses III died before the trial ended, his son and successor, Ramses IV, saw that justice was served. Most of those tried received the death penalty, with six offenders forced to take their own lives right there in the court. Four lucky men walked away with a lesser punishment—they merely had their ears and noses amputated.

History Lesson: Might makes right.

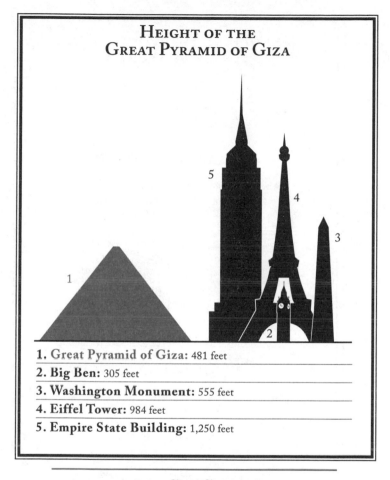

HEIGHT OF THE GREAT PYRAMID OF GIZA

1. Great Pyramid of Giza: 481 feet

2. Big Ben: 305 feet

3. Washington Monument: 555 feet

4. Eiffel Tower: 984 feet

5. Empire State Building: 1,250 feet

Nota Bene

Each side of the base of the Great Pyramid of Giza measures 756 feet. It covers a total area of 13 acres, or the equivalent of about five and a half soccer fields.

DEADLIEST WEAPONS OF THE ANCIENT WORLD

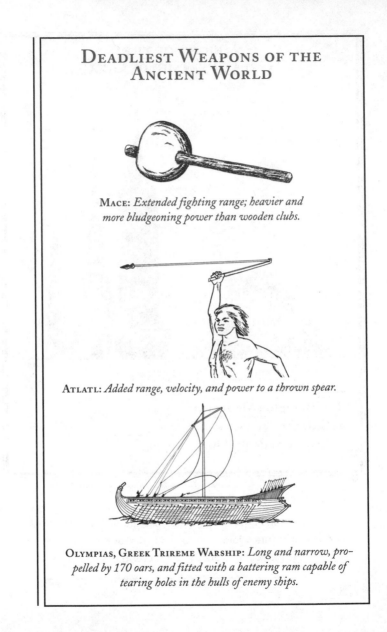

MACE: *Extended fighting range; heavier and more bludgeoning power than wooden clubs.*

ATLATL: *Added range, velocity, and power to a thrown spear.*

OLYMPIAS, GREEK TRIREME WARSHIP: *Long and narrow, propelled by 170 oars, and fitted with a battering ram capable of tearing holes in the hulls of enemy ships.*

PERSIANS TAKE THERMOPYLAE

In 480 BC, 4,000 Greek soldiers clashed with more than 200,000 Persian warriors at Thermopylae, a 6 1/2-foot-wide mountain passage that was critical to the Persian invasion of central Greece. If the Greeks could hold Thermopylae, the Persians would be blocked from further expansion into Greece by the sea on one side and mountains on the other. On the first and second days of fighting, the Persians were bewildered—the tiny Greek contingent easily repelled two attacks, including an onslaught of 10,000 elite fighters. But after the second day's battle, a greedy Greek citizen named Epialtes approached the Persian king and told him of a mountain path that would allow the Persians to encircle and destroy the Greek force from behind. The Persians crossed the mountain overnight, and on the third morning of the battle they annihilated all the Greeks who remained to fight. Epialtes never got the reward he sought with his betrayal—instead of collecting money from the Persians, a price was put on his head by his fellow countrymen. He was forced to flee to Thessaly, where he was eventually murdered.

History Lesson: Traitors seldom prosper, but their benefactors do.

HUMANS TAKE OVER

Year	Population
10,000 BC	1 million
1000 BC	50 million
500 BC	100 million
AD 1	170 million
AD 1000	254 million
AD 1500	425 million
AD 1800	813 million
AD 1900	1.55 billion
AD 1950	2.4 billion
AD 2000	6.07 billion

HOW TO DEFEAT THE EGYPTIAN CHARIOT CORPS IN BATTLE

1 Choose a rocky or hilly terrain for your battle.
To gain the best advantage, stage the skirmish on rocky, sandy, or uneven terrain, where the chariots can easily overturn and break.

2 Close ranks.
Attacking chariots will usually travel abreast, with considerable distance between each of the chariots; the spacing allows them to make quick turns once they have broken through the enemy line so they can strike from the rear. Attack with your flanking troops to force the chariots close together and limit their maneuverability. Do not allow the chariots to break through the line, scatter the infantry, and turn and assault your flanks.

3 Run toward the oncoming chariots at full speed.
Though the Egyptian archers will be barraging your troops with arrows, charge the line of chariots at top speed to prevent them from reaching a full gallop.

4 Attack the driver first, then the archer.
Egyptian chariots are manned by a driver, who wields a whip and holds the horses' reins, and an archer. Attempt to overturn the chariots by using your arrows and spears against the driver to make him lose control of the horses and the vehicle. Do not attempt to damage the chariot's

Charge the oncoming chariots at full speed. Aim spear and arrow attacks at the enemy drivers.

wheels; they are extremely heavy and unlikely to be harmed by your weapons.

5 If the chariots succeed in breaking your line, attack the runners.

Chariot runners—soldiers with spears and swords—may follow the chariot line in formation, killing the wounded and attempting to rescue their own injured troops. Immediately assault the runners with arrows and swords.

Nota Bene

Chariots were used in warfare from 2000 to 1000 BC, when they were replaced by more flexible mounted cavalry units. However, chariots continued to be used for sport for centuries to come; chariot racing was a main draw during the Olympic Games of ancient Greece, and the races were such a popular part of the Roman Circus Games that chariot racers were as famous during their time as today's sports superstars.

ASTYAGES
King of the Medes

BEST KNOWN FOR: Despotic rule • Causing fall of the Median Empire • Ordering the murder of his baby grandson, Cyrus—years later, when Astyages discovered his grandson was still alive, he forced the servant who spared the boy's life to eat his own son

BORN: c. 585 BC; name means "sacker of the cities" in Greek

FAMILY: Son and successor of King Cyaxares. Had more than one wife. Arranged marriage to Aryenis, sister of Lydian king; had daughter, Mandane, with another wife. Mandane bore grandson Cyrus the Great, who vanquished his grandfather in 550 BC, creating the Persian Empire.

LEAST KNOWN FOR: After being overthrown by Cyrus, was granted clemency and allowed to live out his days, possibly even as a governor of Parthia

DEATH: c. 540 BC, possibly murdered or died in prison

EMPIRE BUILDING

THE CLASSICAL WORLD

490 BC   Battle of Marathon; 1,000 Greeks defeat 100,000 Persians

431 BC   Peloponnesian War begins

430 BC   Typhoid fever ravages Athens; 30,000 die

399 BC   Socrates chooses hemlock poisoning over exile after conviction for corrupting Athenian youth

323 BC   Alexander the Great dies at age 32

264 BC   Roman gladiators' first public combats

241 BC   Carthage loses first Punic War

216 BC   Hannibal's army massacres 70,000 Roman soldiers despite being outnumbered 90,000 to 50,000

213 BC   Chinese Emperor Qin Shi Huang-di orders all books burned except those not dealing with agriculture, medicine, prognostication, or himself

202 BC   Silk Road connects China to Roman empire; spreads disease across continents

200 BC   Great Wall of China finished; 1 million killed in unsafe working conditions during construction

170 BC   Streets paved

169 BC   First potholes in streets

140 BC   *Venus of Milo* sculpted

73 BC	Spartacus leads slave revolt
44 BC	Julius Caesar assassinated
30 BC	Marc Antony falls on sword, dies
30 BC	Cleopatra clutches poisonous asp to chest, dies
AD 14	Tiberius, bloodiest Roman emperor, takes power
AD 59	Nero has mother killed
AD 62	Nero has wife Octavia killed; immediately remarries
AD 65	Nero orders Seneca to commit suicide
AD 68	Nero lonely, commits suicide
AD 79	Mt. Vesuvius erupts, 10,000–20,000 die
AD 100	Pyramid of the Sun built in Mexico; includes altar at its peak for ritual human sacrifice
AD 391	Huns introduce pants to Roman Empire; replace togas as daily attire
AD 410	Visigoths ransack Rome
AD 433	Attila the Hun begins 20-year pillage of Europe
AD 476	German Odoacer deposes Emperor Romulus Augustulus; Roman Empire ends
AD 542	Plague ravages Europe; continues for 52 years, halving population
AD 600	Nazca and Moche cultures of South America end after 30-year drought followed by 30 years of flooding

LOWLY GAULS BUTCHER ROMAN NOBLEMEN

In 390 BC, the Gauls successfully entered Rome after crushing the Roman army at the River Allia. With the Roman defenders all scurrying away or slaughtered, the city was eerily empty and quiet. The only Romans on the street were wealthy nobles, who stood in front of their enormous homes dressed in their best attire as a show of their intractable spirit. The barbarian Gauls were initially confused by the Romans' appearance and left the aristocrats alone—until one of them asked a simple question of Marcus Papirius. Papirius, apparently affronted that such a lowly man would dare speak to him, whacked the Gaul in the head with his scepter. The Gauls, confused no longer, butchered Papirius and the rest of the nobles before burning and looting the city.

History Lesson: Never deliver the first punch.

WORST DISASTERS OF THE CLASSICAL WORLD		
Event	Year	Death Toll
Plague of Constantinople	AD 542	300,000
Antioch Earthquake	AD 526	250,000
Massacre of Romans in Asia Minor	88 BC	100,000
Plague of Orosius	AD 125	100,000

HOW TO BUILD A BATTERING RAM

1 Chop down a live hardwood tree.
Use an ax to fell an ash, oak, or elm tree at least 18 inches in diameter.

2 Trim the trunk into a 10- to 12-foot log.
Measure from the bottom of the trunk so you are creating a ram from the thickest, sturdiest part of the tree.

3 Remove all branches from the log.

4 Cover the stump end of the tree with an iron "cap."
Secure the cap to the tree with an iron band, or drive iron spikes through the cap and into the wood.

5 Loop several thick ropes or chains around the ram, several feet apart.

6 Attach the tops of the chains to the center beam of a wheeled, wooden ram tower.
The tower should be at least 8 feet high and as long as the ram. Position the ram inside the tower so that it hangs up off the ground and, when pushed by the ram operators, can swing freely from front to back.

7 Place the ram tower against a door or portcullis.
The capped end of the ram should be positioned against the target.

Pull back on the log, then push it forward and use its momentum to break through the door.

8 Swing the ram against the target until it collapses. Battering rams are typically operated by four to six ram operators who swing the ram in unison to increase momentum and power. Pull back on the hanging log in time with the other operators, then push it forward, allowing the ram to gain momentum as it swings from back to front. Keep out of the ram's path if your hands should slip as you push the log forward; it will swing backward and, without your hands to control it, it may knock you down.

Be Aware
A ram tower with a metal roof will prevent arrows from hitting the ram operators.

ALEXANDER INTRODUCES UNORTHODOX BATTLE TACTICS

In 331 BC, Persia put up a strong defense to stop Alexander the Great's advancing Macedonian army. King Darius of Persia amassed an enormous army to confront the young warrior, including more than 250,000 men, elephants, a giant cavalry, and a battalion of chariots. Alexander, whose army had fewer than 50,000 soldiers, was undaunted by the vastness of the Persian force. He first sent a wave of attacking soldiers to the Persians' right flank, causing an imbalance on the line; then, when enough of the Persian troops were occupied on the right, Alexander sent everyone else to attack the center, causing mass confusion on the Persians' part and leading to an absolute rout. The death toll tells the story—Persian army: 90,000. Macedonians: Fewer than 500. Alexander's strategy has been studied and copied ever since.

History Lesson: Innovation is the key to success.

DEATHS OF GREAT RELIGIOUS/PHILOSOPHICAL LEADERS

Name	Cause of Death
Buddha (563–483 BC)	Natural causes; ate a mushroom delicacy and died between two Sal trees
Confucius (551–479 BC)	Old age
Socrates (470–399 BC)	Suicide by hemlock poisoning. Convicted of corrupting the youth of Athens; chooses poison over exile.
Plato (427–347 BC)	Old age
Aristotle (384–322 BC)	Stomach ailment
Jesus (approx. 8–2 BC–AD 29–36)	Crucified by the Romans
Mohammed (AD 570–632)	Possible poisoning. Complained of a bad headache and was bedridden for several days before dying.

STUDENT AS MASTER

CHANDRA GUPTA AVENGES PROFESSOR

As a young professor, Chanakya, one of the world's greatest political thinkers, studied under King Dhana Nanda in Pataliputra until he and the king had a minor dispute and the king dismissed him from the court. A proud man, he vowed his revenge on the petty and corrupt king. Thus, several years later, when he met the intelligent, resourceful prince Chandra Gupta, he saw a chance to make good on his pledge. Chanakya enrolled the prince at his university and took him under his wing. Together, they planned to oust the king, forming a vast army with the help of the Himalayan King, Parvatka. In 322 BC, they vanquished King Dhana, and Chandra Gupta became the first true emperor of India with Chanakya at his side.

History Lesson: Be nice to the "little people."

GREAT WALL OF CHINA VS. BERLIN WALL

	Great Wall of China	Berlin Wall
Dimensions	35 feet high, 4,600 miles long	12 feet high, 103 miles long
Materials	Granite, earth, stone, brick	Concrete blocks, barbed wire, electric fence
Time to Build	2,000 years (400 BC–AD 1600)	1 night (August 12–13, 1961); perfected over time
Purpose	Protect China from invaders	Stop communist East Germans from defecting to capitalist West Germany
Number of Guard Stations	about 500	302
Successful Because	Never breached	Stopped talented young professionals from moving to West Germany
Failed Because	Internal rebellions allowed Mongols and Manchurians to take power without destroying the Wall	More than 5,000 people tunneled under or climbed or flew over the Wall

QIN SHI HUANG-DI EMPEROR OF CHINA MONTHS AFTER DEATH

Chinese emperor Qin Shi Huang-di was the strong personality holding a troubled kingdom together. After ascending to the throne in 238 BC, he and his generals worked furiously to unite the divided country for the first time. In addition to building the Great Wall of China, he abolished feudalism, forced aristocrats to move to the capital city of Xian, and standardized weights, measures, language, and law—all reforms that angered many of the country's elite. When the emperor died while traveling through Eastern China in 210 BC, his prime minister, Li Si, hoped to put off a revolt by keeping his death a secret. During the two-month journey back to Xian, Li Si entered the emperor's wagon each morning and pretended to discuss various state affairs with Qin's corpse. To counter the increasingly potent and horrific smell of the emperor's decaying body, Li Si had wagons of fish placed directly before and after the emperor's. At the end of their journey back to the capital, Li Si announced the death of the emperor. Fighting broke out immediately, and within four years, Qin's dynasty had collapsed.

History Lesson: You can't put off the inevitable.

Nota Bene

Qin Shi is buried in a 20-square-mile underground palace with more than 6,000 terra-cotta soldiers and horses, chariots made of wood and bronze, iron farm implements, bronze and leather bridles, bows and arrows, spears, and swords. The army faces east, guarding the emperor's tomb from his adversaries.

HOW TO SURVIVE AN ASP BITE

1 Locate the site of the injury.
The entry wound may be small, it may appear that the skin has not been broken, or there may be just a single fang puncture.

2 Remove all jewelry.
A bite to the hand may result in severe swelling, and bracelets, rings, and watches will restrict blood flow, ultimately requiring amputation of the limb.

3 If possible, lower the location of the bite beneath the level of the heart.

4 Rinse the bite with water.

5 Cut a narrow strip of cloth.

6 Tie the cloth around the limb 2 to 4 inches above the wound.
Do not tie the cloth too tightly; you should easily be able to fit a finger underneath it. The band should not cut arterial blood flow to the injury site.

7 Suction venom from the wound.
Use a bellows to suction unabsorbed venom from the wound. Do not use your mouth to suck out the venom, as the poison may enter your bloodstream.

You should be able to fit your finger underneath the cloth tourniquet.

Be Aware

- Most poisonous snake bites are not fatal, and death (when it occurs) typically takes hours or days, even when the victim is left untreated.
- A small amount of injected venom—combined with the size and general health of the victim—can result in moderate symptoms, including swelling, pain, and a burning sensation at the injury site; thirst and chills; and nausea. Larger amounts of hemotoxin may cause rapid heartbeat, low blood pressure, shallow breathing, convulsions, and respiratory failure.
- Fatty tissue absorbs venom more slowly than muscle.

Now We Know

Antivenin, based on the vaccine concept developed by Louis Pasteur, was invented in the late nineteenth century and is now used to treat many types of poisonous snakebites.

HANNIBAL LEADS TROOPS ACROSS SNOWY ALPS

In 218 BC, Hannibal found a way to take the Romans by surprise—by crossing into Italy through the Alps. Unfortunately, he and his bedraggled Carthaginian army of 48,000 men arrived at the foot of the mountains in mid-October, just as winter was setting in. Crossing the Alps in the snow is a difficult task for any army, but Hannibal's men were mostly from the warm climes of Northern Africa and were unprepared for the brutally cold conditions. Additionally, they faced constant attack from Celts on the narrow, winding mountain pathways. Hannibal's army sustained a high casualty rate during their 15-day march across the Alps, with less than half of his men making it to Italy. However, once they were there, they easily defeated the small army of Publius Cornelius Scipio, who was left without reinforcements because the Roman armies expected the war to be fought in Iberia and Africa. Later, Hannibal convinced Gaul's army to join his, bolstering his forces while the Romans waited for help in their own country. Though the Carthaginians ultimately lost the war, Hannibal continued the battle for more than 15 years, appearing invincible until the very end.

History Lesson: Always expect the unexpected.

Nota Bene

Early in Hannibal's march to Rome, he faced the problem of getting his 37 elephants across the Rhône River. The water was too deep for them to wade, and the animals refused to board boats. Hannibal instructed his men to build several large rafts and to tie them together to make a floating pier, then cover the top of the pier with soil to make the elephants think they were still on land. Once the animals were on the pier, the ropes securing it to the river bank were cut, and Hannibal's boats towed the elephants across to the other side.

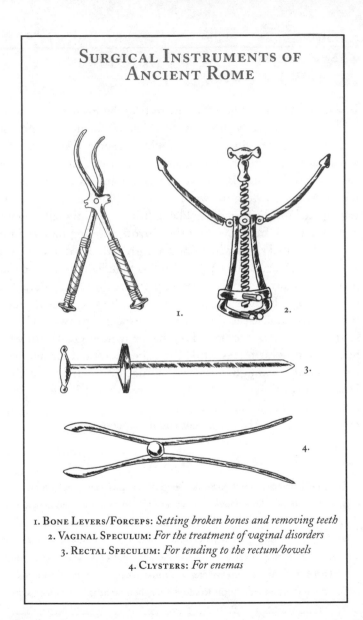

SURGICAL INSTRUMENTS OF ANCIENT ROME

1. **BONE LEVERS/FORCEPS:** *Setting broken bones and removing teeth*
2. **VAGINAL SPECULUM:** *For the treatment of vaginal disorders*
3. **RECTAL SPECULUM:** *For tending to the rectum/bowels*
4. **CLYSTERS:** *For enemas*

SPARTACUS RETURNS TO ITALY

After leading a successful slave revolt against the Romans in 73 BC, Spartacus led his army of 90,000 men to the brink of escape into Gaul. But at the threshold of freedom, he was persuaded by his men to turn back into Italy to reap more plunder. This proved to be a disastrous decision; the Romans had amassed an army capable of putting down the revolt. They killed Spartacus, defeated his army, and then, as a warning to any others who might try to challenge Roman authority, they crucified 6,000 of the recaptured slaves along the Appian Way and left their bodies to rot for years afterward.

History Lesson: Quit when you're ahead.

WHO HAD IT WORSE?		
	Moses	Spartacus
Title	Leader of the Jewish slaves	Leader of the gladiator slaves
Enemy	Egyptian Pharaoh	Crassus, Roman general
Inspiration	God	Jaunus Maximi, fellow gladiator
Number of Slaves	600,000	100,000
Initial Weapons	God's plagues	Knives from kitchen at gladiator school
Safe Haven	Israel	Gaul
Hardships	Leading people through desert for 40 years	Fighting Romans at every turn with ragtag army
Bad Turning Point	Striking the rock God asked him to speak to	Turning back from Gaul to plunder Italy first
End Result	Sees promised land, but not allowed to live there	Killed by Romans at the river Silarus; 6,000 of his followers crucified and left to rot

CALIGULA

Gaius Caesar Germanicus, Roman Emperor

BEST KNOWN FOR: Sexual relationships with his sisters, in addition to his four wives • Thinking himself a god; ordering his statue to be erected in the Temple in Jerusalem • Opening a brothel in the Roman palace • Leading a military campaign in Gaul wherein he ordered soldiers to collect seashells as the "spoils of the conquered ocean"

BORN: AD 12, in the Julio-Claudian resort of Antium

FAMILY: Accompanied his parents on military campaigns as a baby, wearing a miniature soldier's outfit. Father died when he was seven; mother and older brothers arrested and died in custody when he was a teenager.

PHYSICAL DESCRIPTION: Tall and thin, with long legs and sunken eyes. Though he had thinning hair on his head, his body was hairy.

LEAST KNOWN FOR: His generosity and generally decent behavior when he first became ruler; it wasn't until after a severe sickness seven months into his reign that he developed delusions of divinity

FAVORITE PET: A racehorse named Incitatus, who lived inside the palace in a stable box of carved ivory, dressed in purple blankets and collars of precious stones

DEATH: January 24, AD 41, murdered in a conspiracy enacted by officers of the Praetorian Guard, who ambushed him outside his chambers, then murdered his fourth wife and baby daughter

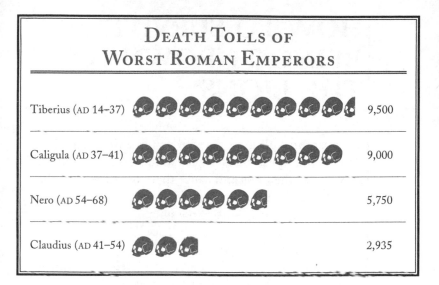

DEATH TOLLS OF WORST ROMAN EMPERORS	
Tiberius (AD 14–37)	9,500
Caligula (AD 37–41)	9,000
Nero (AD 54–68)	5,750
Claudius (AD 41–54)	2,935

BACKFIRE

ROMANS UNDERESTIMATE THE BRITS

Thinking a quick humiliation would take all the fight out of the British, Roman soldiers under the rule of Emperor Nero flogged British queen Boudicca and raped her two daughters in front of her shortly after the death of her husband, King Prasutagus, in AD 60. But instead of causing the queen to withdraw in fear, the soldiers' actions had the opposite effect. Boudicca rallied a surly army of rebels to attack the Romans at every turn, ultimately killing 70,000 Romans and pro-Roman Britons. They nearly succeeded in wiping the Romans out of Britain before finally succumbing to them at the Battle of Watling Street.

History Lesson: Don't gratuitously antagonize your enemy.

HOW TO SURVIVE BEING THROWN TO THE LIONS

1 Remove your animal skin clothing.
Your captors will have covered you in animal blood or dressed you in the skins of prey animals; such garments may arouse the lions and cause them to attack. Use the skins to wipe off the blood and immediately move as far from the discarded skins as possible.

2 Do not provoke the lions.
If the lions appear sick, sedate, distracted, or disinterested, do not approach them, or you risk inciting an attack that is not forthcoming. Though the lions will have been starved in preparation for your confrontation, there is no certainty that the beasts in the arena will attack you. If the animals don't become aggressive, your fight may be rescheduled for another day's circus games, sparing your life at least until the following day.

3 Fight an animal handler to secure a weapon.
If the lions appear agitated, use your bare hands to attack the smallest, weakest-looking animal handler (*bestiarii*) in the arena. Procure his whip, sword, shield, and/or other protective gear.

4 Watch for mock charges.
A lion may make several mock charges before actually attacking. It will run forward suddenly, then stop. It may

Remove any animal skins. Yell to discourage the lion from charging.

back away before charging again. Mock-charging is an indication that a real attack is imminent. Stand your ground and be ready.

5 Yell.
Shout as loud as you can. Lions are sensitive to loud noises, and yelling may discourage one from further charges. Yelling will also act as an impressive display of strength for the crowd in the arena.

6 If you are unable to prevent an attack, use the sword to fight the animal.
Push the lion's paws and head away from you, thrusting the sword into its abdomen.

7 Behave courageously.
Though the animals are typically the victors in cases of *damnatio ad bestias* ("condemnation to the beasts"), the outcome is not always certain. A particularly brave fight leading to victory in the arena may grant you a temporary reprieve or, possibly, a pardon.

Be Aware

- There are wooden doors set into the dirt floor; these doors may lead to passageways or empty animal cages that can provide some measure of protection from lions already in the arena. Do not open the doors in an attempt to escape. The cages may still have vicious, live animals in them, and even an empty cage is only a temporary refuge. You will be pulled out and forced to continue the fight, but since you attempted to hide rather than facing your challenge head-on, it will be impossible to receive a pardon or reprieve even if you are victorious against the animals in the arena.

- You may be able to keep the animals at bay by cracking a whip stolen from a *bestiarii*. Circle the whip as far above your head as you can while still allowing for smooth movement. Keep your back straight and your elbow slightly bent to ensure a smooth motion, with your opposite arm out to the side to give you balance. Make one large circle overhead and then a quick upright S approximately 2 feet in front of you, keeping your wrist at a 45-degree angle to your body as you bring the whip down and complete the motion. Wherever you follow through with your wrist is where the tip—the most dangerous part of the whip—will go.

Nota Bene

Roman criminals were thrown into the arena to suffer a public execution by facing animals such as lions, leopards, or bears. The animals were starved before being released into the arena to encourage their attack. The criminals were not given a weapon with which to fight the animals.

ROMANS TEACH ATTILA HOW TO DEFEAT THEM

As part of an exchange meant to foster peace between the Romans and the Huns, 12-year-old Attila was taken into the Roman Court in AD 418 and shown the life of a Roman noble. The Romans hoped he would take his knowledge of their social customs and integrate their ways into the Huns' tribal lifestyle. Instead, Attila studied their military maneuvers and rigid political system. Shortly after he and his brother, Blenda, were named leaders of the Huns in 434, young Attila used his knowledge of Roman politics and methods against them, negotiating a peace treaty highly advantageous to the Huns. In 445, Attila murdered his brother and became the sole ruler of the Hun empire, and thereafter he and his army fought the Romans in Eastern Europe. Attila won victory upon victory, until he met his match in Roman general Flavius Aetius—who, ironically, had spent time with the Huns as part of the same child exchange that had taken young Attila to Rome.

History Lesson: Indoctrinating others in your beliefs may teach them more than you know.

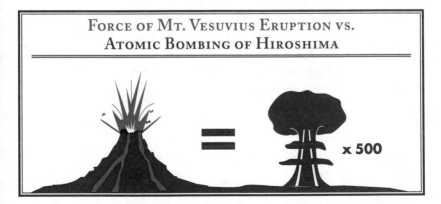

FORCE OF MT. VESUVIUS ERUPTION VS. ATOMIC BOMBING OF HIROSHIMA

= x 500

ATTILA THE HUN
King of the Huns

BEST KNOWN FOR: Plundering Germanic nations • Sending troops as mercenary forces to fight against Eastern Roman Empire • Invading Eastern Roman Empire, Northern Italy, and Gaul • Creating peace treaties that extorted funds from subjugated nations for years afterward

BORN: AD 406

FAMILY: Sent as a child to the Roman court of Emperor Honorius as a peace offering. Murdered brother in 445 to gain sole leadership of Huns.

PHYSICAL DESCRIPTION: Short, with a broad chest, large head, thin beard, and small, beady eyes

EDUCATION: Schooled in the Roman Empire, where he studied Roman internal politics, foreign policies, leadership techniques, and protocols

FIRST JOB: Shared kingship of the Huns with his brother Bleda

NICKNAME: Scourge of God

LEAST KNOWN FOR: Modesty of dress and style. Drank out of a wooden cup, wore clean but casual dress when not in battle.

QUOTE: In speaking about his military conquests, "Where my horse has trodden, no grass grows."

DEATH: 453. After celebrating his marriage, Attila suffered a severe nosebleed and choked to death in a drunken stupor. Buried in a coffin of gold, silver, and iron. His funeral party was killed immediately after his burial so the location would remain secret.

DUNGEONS AND DRAGONS

THE MIDDLE AGES

526 Antioch earthquake kills 250,000 religious pilgrims

537 Arthur, King of the Britons, killed in Battle of Camlan

615 "Burning water" (petroleum) used in lamps in Japan

641 Book-reproducing industry at Alexandria destroyed; end of Alexandrian school, center of Western culture

663 Islam splits over leadership, Sunni and Shia sects form

671 Greek Fire first used by Byzantines

791 Byzantine Emperor Constantine imprisons his mother, Irene, for her cruelty

797 Byzantine Empress Irene captures and blinds her son, Constantine; seizes control of empire

c. 800 First castles built in Europe

814 Charlemagne dies; European culture regresses

860 Viking ships raid Constantinople

1052 William the Conqueror "proposes" to Matilda of Flanders by tracking her down, dragging her off her horse, and throwing her into the street. She accepts.

1076 Roman Catholic Church begins burning of heretics

1101 First Crusade succeeds; Christians claim Jerusalem

1149	Second Crusade fails
1170	Thomas à Becket, Archbishop of Canterbury, murdered by knights of King Henry II
1170	Rat traps invented
1192	Third Crusade fails
1201	Earthquake kills 1.1 million Syrians; deadliest quake in history
1202	Court jesters appear in Europe
1204	Fourth Crusade fails
1212	Children's Crusade fails
1219	Genghis Khan demolishes cities and slaughters civilians in central Asia, Afghanistan, Persia, and Russia
1221	Fifth Crusade fails
1291	Christians lose city of Acre; Crusades over
1297	Moas, giant giraffe birds of New Zealand, extinct
1307	Philip the Fair tortures and burns Knights Templar at the stake to avoid paying his debt to them
1315	Europe's Great Famine begins; 10 to 25 percent of population dead in two years
1347	Black Death begins, kills 20 to 30 million in five years
1431	Joan of Arc burned at stake
1441	First shipment of African slaves to Portugal
1453	Hundred Years' War ends after 117 years

HOW TO DEFEND A CASTLE AGAINST A SIEGE

1 Counterattack with archers.
Fire arrows from arrow loops (slits in the wall) as soon as the enemy is within range (a little over 200 yards).

2 Keep the moat filled with water.
A deep, full moat will render battering rams—which must be pushed directly against a wall—ineffective. It will also deter sappers (tunnelers) from digging underneath the outer walls of the castle, stabilizing the tunnel with timber, and setting the wood on fire to collapse the walls from underneath. Attackers will attempt to fill the moat with soil, rocks, and timber to facilitate their crossing, so the deeper the moat the better.

3 Attack from above.
Pour hot oil, boiling water, or burning oil mixed with sand (to penetrate armor) onto attackers scaling castle walls with ladders.

4 Protect the drawbridge.
The enemy will try to enter the castle at its most vulnerable point—the drawbridge. Reinforce the position above the drawbridge with extra archers and soldiers. Station additional soldiers inside the drawbridge to engage in ground combat should your other efforts fail.

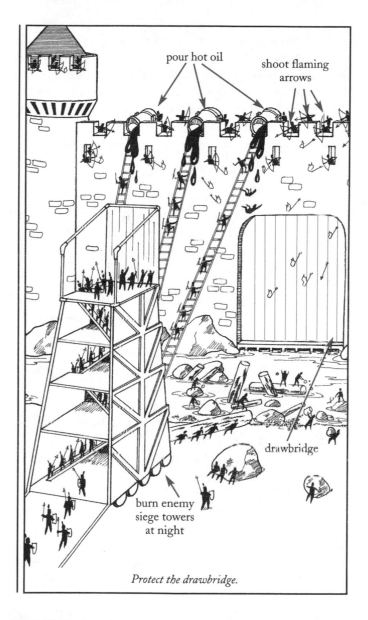

pour hot oil

shoot flaming arrows

drawbridge

burn enemy siege towers at night

Protect the drawbridge.

5 Shoot flaming arrows at siege towers.

The enemy may build a siege tower, a tall, hollow, wooden structure that can be filled with soldiers and wheeled to the castle wall. Once there, ladders, ropes, or a drawbridge at the top of the tower are used to span the moat and allow enemy soldiers to reach the wall. Defend against the tower by bombarding it with fire arrows or firepots (pots filled with flaming tar).

6 Destroy siege engines.

Under cover of darkness, slip from the castle and set fire to partially constructed trebuchets or siege towers to prevent their use in battle.

Be Aware

- Always keep a stockpile of food and weapons within the castle walls. If you receive advance warning that a siege will occur, evacuate the lord and lady of the castle as well as women and children. Sieges can be more of a waiting game than a battle, with the attacking army creating a blockade to prevent anyone from entering or leaving. If the castle is well stocked, the enemy may eventually withdraw to escape the elements.

- Besieged castle dwellers can sometimes ward off a deadly attack by negotiating a timeframe for surrender with the enemy. For example, a constable may offer to surrender the castle to an attacking army if the lord does not send reinforcements within a specific time period. This arrangement can benefit both sides because it not only keeps the castle intact, it also saves the attacking army the effort and cost of waging battle.

DEADLIEST WEAPONS OF THE MIDDLE AGES

GREEK FIRE: *Napalm-like substance used by the Byzantines, especially in naval battles, since it would burn even on water.*

ENGLISH LONGBOW: *Later know as the "Medieval machine gun" because of its range and quick-firing possibility, had an effective killing range of up to 250 yards.*

TREBUCHET: *A large catapult, useful for hurling everything from boulders to burning rags to plague-ridden corpses over walls and embankments.*

GUNPOWDER/CANNON: *Long range and destructive; gave smaller armies with the technology a fighting chance against larger armies without it.*

GREEKS LOSE THEIR SECRET WEAPON

When it was invented in 673, Greek Fire was the pinnacle of warfare technology. Used by the Byzantines in battles against the Muslims, this "liquid fire" stuck to any surface, spontaneously ignited, and burned ferociously, even on water. The mixture was pumped through a tube and siphoned onto the enemy with devastating results, especially in naval battles—a single confrontation in 678 cost the Muslims more than 30,000 lives. The Byzantines' use of Greek Fire in defending Constantinople forced the Muslim Caliph to turn back time and again; legends of the weapon became widespread, so that the very appearance of a tube could force an enemy to retreat. Because it was so effective, the Byzantines closely guarded the recipe, living in fear that it would fall into enemy hands. But shortly after an encounter with the Muslims in 718, the Byzantines lost their precious formula. No one in Byzantium was able to re-create the concoction, and without their weapon of choice, the Byzantines lost their advantage. Though variants of Greek Fire were later developed by the Arabs, none of the re-creations was ever as potent or as effective as the original. Its exact chemical makeup remains a mystery to this day.

History Lesson: Back up your data.

WORST DISASTERS OF THE MIDDLE AGES

Event	Year	Death Toll
Black Death	1347–1351	25 million
Syrian Earthquake	1201	1.1 million
Egyptian Famine	1200–1202	600,000
Constantinople Plague	542	300,000
Antioch Earthquake	526	250,000
Japanese Famine	1181	100,000

Y1K

WORLD SCHEDULED TO END

European religious zealots were convinced that the year 1000 would bring the second coming of Christ and the end of the world, as had been predicted for centuries. Despite disavowals by the Church, hordes of desperate pilgrims traveled to Jerusalem for the event, with many giving away their property and possessions in the hope of guaranteeing themselves a place in heaven. Thousands died of starvation along the way, and religious paranoia increased to epic levels: Shooting stars and even thunderstorms were interpreted as signs of the apocalypse. On the last day of the millennium, throngs of people clambered up Mount Zion, eagerly anticipating the return of Jesus, but the day came and went without his arrival. When it became clear that nothing was going to happen, the long-suffering pilgrims made the journey home. Upon their return, most of those who hadn't given away their property before leaving found their homes so degraded from lack of upkeep during their several-year absence that they were forced to rebuild from scratch.

History Lesson: Don't get swept up in apocalyptic panic.

HOW TO SURVIVE A JOUST

1 Don your armor.
The ideal armor for a joust is curved and smooth to help deflect your opponent's lance, with extra protection on your left side, which will be closest to your opponent and the most likely place for him to strike.

2 Mount your steed.
Sit hard in the saddle. Place your feet into the stirrups and use your knees to steady yourself on your horse in preparation for collision with your opponent's lance.

3 At the signal, spur your horse forward.
Hold your lance in your right hand, perpendicular to the ground, and guide your horse ahead, on the left side of the tilt barrier. Lean forward slightly to increase your visibility; the narrow eye slot in your helmet will impair your vision.

4 At the last possible moment, lower your lance toward your opponent.
Extend the lance over your horse's left shoulder at a 35-degree angle across your body.

5 Aim your lance low on your opponent's breastplate.
Though your ultimate goal is to knock your opponent off his horse to win the match, you can also score points by striking your opponent on his helmet (2 points) or on his breastplate or shield (1 point).

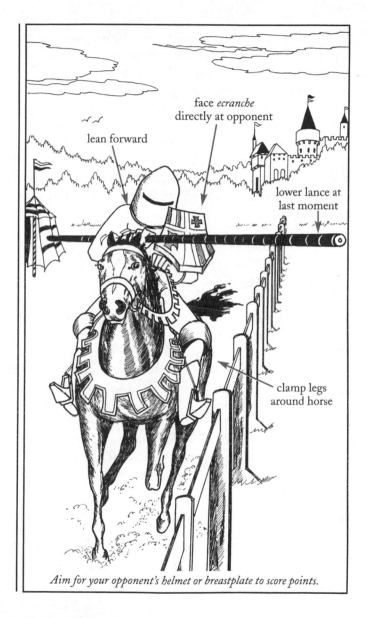

face *ecranche*
directly at opponent

lean forward

lower lance at
last moment

clamp legs
around horse

Aim for your opponent's helmet or breastplate to score points.

6 Hold your *ecranche* directly facing the impending impact to disperse the force of your opponent's lance. Your shield, or *ecranche,* will be attached to your chest or your left shoulder. Hold your rein hand just ahead of the front of the saddle and rest your knuckles on or just above the ridge between the horse's shoulder bones. Do not allow the *ecranche* to sit so high that it scoops upward, or your opponent's lance will slide up to hit your helmet. Note that defensive moves, such as ducking or weaving, are not allowed and will result in a loss of points.

7 Lean backward on impact.
Use your legs like a vise around your horse to remain in your saddle. Meeting force with force, at a slight angle, will diffuse the power of the strike (equal to the force of a blow from a blacksmith's hammer). If you are knocked from your steed, immediately tuck and roll. If possible, angle your fall so that you land on your shoulder and roll with—don't resist—your forward momentum once you strike the ground. The weight of your armor will stop you quickly enough.

8 Repeat steps 3 through 7 until either you or your opponent are knocked from the saddle.

Be Aware
The rules for each joust differ from tournament to tournament, though typically each match consists of several warm-up runs, called "measuring passes," followed by three to six contacting passes.

Who Had It Worse?

	Eunuch	Court Jester
Also Known As	Castrato	Fool
Noteworthy Characteristics	Castrated	Often deformed, dwarfed, or crippled; incessant laughter
Duties	Guarding or serving in harems or women's chambers; chamberlain to kings	Entertaining, poking fun at king and court; bringing good luck
Attire	Varies from court to court	Three-pointed hat with bells at the tips, mock scepter, motley coat
Misconception	They can't have sex	They are total imbeciles
Heroes	Ly Thuong Kiet, a eunuch turned general in Vietnam, wrote the first Vietnamese Declaration of Independence	Archibald "Archy" Armstrong gained influence with King James VI while annoying everyone in the court

Nota Bene

In the earliest recorded jousts, opponents battled to kill one another, but during the thirteenth century, tournaments became contests of skill more than fights to the death. Jousters were protected by specialized armor and the "lance of peace," which was either blunted or topped with a crown-shaped head to disperse its impact. However, for serious challenges and combat, sharpened weaponry and heavy field armor were still used; these contests ended only when one participant was killed or disabled.

VIKINGS BANNED FROM NEW WORLD

Early in the 11th century, the Vikings arrived in what would later be known as Nova Scotia, dubbing it Vinland. Viking ruler Leif Eriksson left his sister Freydis in charge of colonizing the new territory, but her first settlement attempts were beaten back by the natives. Returning in 1013 with a better-armed fleet, Freydis was upset to discover that two Viking families were already living in the house she planned to claim. In a fury, she ordered them all murdered; when her cohorts refused to kill the women and children, Freydis slaughtered them herself. Word of the massacre spread after some colonists returned home to Greenland, putting Leif in a quandary: For killing innocents, his sister should have been killed, but it was almost as great a sin in Viking culture to kill one's own blood. His solution was to forbid anyone from returning to Vinland again—an edict that denied the Vikings their chance of settling North America.

History Lesson: Nepotism brings its own set of problems.

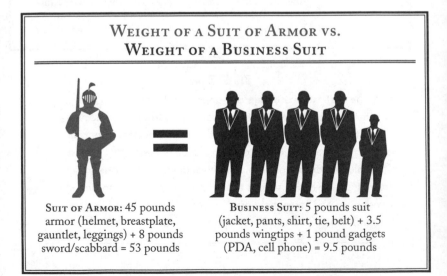

WEIGHT OF A SUIT OF ARMOR VS. WEIGHT OF A BUSINESS SUIT

SUIT OF ARMOR: 45 pounds armor (helmet, breastplate, gauntlet, leggings) + 8 pounds sword/scabbard = 53 pounds

BUSINESS SUIT: 5 pounds suit (jacket, pants, shirt, tie, belt) + 3.5 pounds wingtips + 1 pound gadgets (PDA, cell phone) = 9.5 pounds

CHILDREN'S CRUSADE ENDS IN DISASTER

The Christian crusades to wrest Palestine from Islamic control took an unexpectedly youthful turn in 1212, when a 12-year-old French shepherd named Stephen took up the cause. Claiming divine inspiration, he rallied thousands of his fellow children and sought to succeed where their elders had failed. Marching in the summer heat and depending on charitable handouts, the young crusaders made their way from Vendome in northwestern France nearly 400 miles to Marseilles harbor, where Stephen had predicted that the seas would part. When the seas remained unmoved, the children boarded ships, which set sail not for Palestine as the adults had promised, but to the Algerian coast, where the children were sold into slavery.

Another inspired crusader, a 12-year-old German boy named Nicholas, rallied thousands of German children and young adults in the Rhineland a few weeks after Stephen's crusade began. They embarked on a journey over the Swiss Alps and onward to the Italian coast at Pisa, where they too expected the seas to part (they didn't). Dejected, Nicholas and his remaining followers trooped to Rome for an audience with Pope Innocent, who suggested that they go home. Most (apparently including Nicholas) perished on the journey back, and Nicholas's father was hanged by angry, grieving parents.

History Lesson: Don't rush growing up.

MEDIEVAL CRIME AND PUNISHMENT

Crime	Punishment
Drunkenness	Stocks or a public whipping
Prostitution	A public whipping, followed by a bombardment of rotten fruit and vegetables from the crowd
Minor Thievery	Flogging
Major Thievery	Amputation of hand that committed the crime
Dishonesty/Cheating	Dunking stool and/or stocks
Gossiping	Wearing of muzzle or metal mask with a studded or spiked device that sits on the tongue to prevent speech
Gambling	Wearing a chain decorated with giant wooden cards and bricks
Hunting in Royal Park	Amputation of ears
Late to Church/Falling Asleep During Sermon	Wearing giant rosary around neck
Playing Bad Music	Wearing the "shame flute," an instrument resembling a clarinet that is hung around neck and clamped to fingers

HOW TO SURVIVE IN A DUNGEON

1 | Stay hydrated.
In an underground dungeon made of unfinished stone, water may seep from walls and up from the floor. Use a piece of cloth to absorb the liquid, then squeeze it into your mouth. If your water is rationed, drink when you eat to help aid digestion, then take small sips at regular intervals throughout the day.

2 | Catch insects for food.
Eat grasshoppers (remove the wings first), beetle grubs, termites, and weevils, all of which are good sources of protein. Cockroaches and flies carry dangerous bacteria and should be avoided as food. Do not eat rats and mice unless they are skinned, gutted, and cooked.

3 | Exercise to prevent muscle atrophy.
Even if you are manacled or chained to the wall, keep blood flowing to your extremities by flexing against your bonds and then relaxing, stretching as far as possible. If you are not bound, walk back and forth in the cell and do deep knee bends and push-ups to maintain physical strength.

4 | Keep your mind occupied.
Keep your brain active by remembering pleasurable experiences, down to the smallest details.

Stay active to maintain physical strength.

5 Stay positive.

Never give up hope that your prison sentence will be commuted, or that the castle will be liberated and all the prisoners freed.

Nota Bene

A castle's dungeon, or oubliette, was typically located in its foundations or ground floor. The dungeon had no windows and was accessible only through a hole in the floor above it. The entrance of the dungeon was covered by a trapdoor, and though the potential for a prisoner's escape was slim, a guard slept on top of the trapdoor at night and a large boulder was pushed on top of it during the day. To enter the dungeon, prisoners were tied to a rope and lowered into the room; food was delivered in the same manner. The prisoners were forced to endure total darkness, so by the time many were released (if they were ever released), they had lost their eyesight through lack of use. At this time in history, imprisonment was typically used by a lord to remove threatening opponents, extort ransom, or exact revenge on fellow aristocrats.

SHAH MISJUDGES GENGHIS KHAN

In 1219, the Shah of Khwarezm, Ala' ad-Din Muhammad, thought so little of the ambassadors Genghis Khan had sent to settle a minor dispute between them that he ordered the ambassadors seized. As a gesture meant to humiliate them, he had their beards burned off in front of a crowd of onlookers. When Genghis Khan learned that his emissaries were so mistreated, the Mongol warlord immediately declared war on the region. The Shah was not concerned, since he knew his army of half a million soldiers would far outnumber whatever meager forces the Mongols could advance. What he hadn't counted on, however, was the brutal efficiency and military genius of Genghis Khan and his army. The Mongols wiped out the Shah's army and chased him for thousands of miles, laying waste to his empire all the way. Eventually, alone, terrified, and penniless, the Shah literally died of fright of the oncoming horde. His empire, and the intellectual center of Islam, were destroyed.

History Lesson: Make sure you know what your enemy is capable of before you strike the first blow.

WORST MEDIEVAL BABY NAMES

Male	Female
Ailwin	Amalasuntha
Clovis	Berthefried
Horsa	Earcongota
Hunwald	Hawisa
Lothar	Malota
Thrydwulf	Sexburg
Wuffa	Ultrogotha

GENGHIS KHAN
Mongol Emperor

BEST KNOWN FOR: Creating Mongol Empire • Opening Silk Route • Ruthless battle tactics

BORN: c. 1162, in Hentiy, Mongolia

FAMILY: Father murdered by Tatars; cast out of clan with mother and siblings after father's death; killed his half brother for stealing his fish (age 13); wife was kidnapped by rival Merkit tribe

PHYSICAL DESCRIPTION: Tall, with cat eyes

EDUCATION: Yurt-schooled

FIRST JOB: Goatherd

LEAST KNOWN FOR: His supposed fear of dogs

QUOTE: "Man's greatest good fortune is to chase and defeat his enemy, seize his total possessions, leave his married women weeping and wailing, ride his gelding, and use the bodies of his women."

DEATH: 1227. Buried with 40 horses. Soldiers killed all witnesses to the funeral, including animals, and then killed themselves, so that no living being would know the tomb's location, which is still a mystery.

MONGOL ARMY CONQUERS EUROPE—ALMOST

By 1242, the Mongol army had already conquered much of Russia and was looking to expand its empire westward into Europe. The Mongols had a long history of success under their current leader, Ogedai Khan—Ogedai's son, Batu, who commanded the Mongol armies in the field, had lost only one battle in 20 years. As the Mongols cut a bloody swath through eastern Europe, overtaking Krakow and Poland and finally laying waste to Pest, Hungary's largest city, it seemed that no army could stop them. But on the cusp of the Mongol's charge into Austria and the rest of western Europe, Batu was informed of his father's death, and he and his soldiers withdrew to Mongolia to assure his position in the line of succession. Batu assumed they would return to continue the expansion, but it was not to be: In the intervening years, Europe fortified itself and the Mongol army lost ground, losing the opportunity to expand their empire to the Atlantic.

History Lesson: Decision-making is chance-taking.

SUPERSTITIONS OF THE MIDDLE AGES

Good Luck	Bad Luck
• Touching wood • Making a hole in the bottom of an empty boiled eggshell • Catching falling leaves during autumn • Throwing shoes after someone leaving for a journey	• Peacock feather • Passing someone on the stairs • Putting new shoes on a table • Sneezing

HOW TO TREAT THE BUBONIC PLAGUE

★ Act quickly upon appearance of symptoms.
Death occurs, in most cases, two to four days after symptoms are recognized. Untreated plague is fatal in 30 to 75 percent of all cases, so time is of the essence.

★ Bathe in human urine and wear human excrement.

★ Place dead animals in your home.

★ Use leeches.

★ Drink molten gold or powdered emeralds, eat figs before six in the morning, and do not exercise.

Be Aware
- Symptoms of bubonic or "black" plague include: high fever, shivering, rapid pulse and breathing rate, exhaustion, nausea, vomiting, aching joints, chills, diarrhea, muscular pain, headaches, mental disorganization, giddiness, intolerance to light, a white coating on the tongue, delirium, lymph nodes swollen to the size of chicken eggs (especially in the groin and thigh regions), pustules, and eventually internal bleeding that causes blood to dry under the skin, blackening the flesh.
- Symptoms will appear within a week of exposure. In nonfatal cases, the fever will begin to fall in about five days and will be normal in about two weeks.

Doctor in Plague Gear

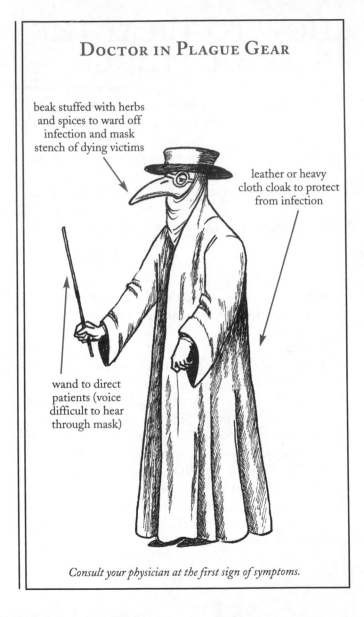

beak stuffed with herbs
and spices to ward off
infection and mask
stench of dying victims

leather or heavy
cloth cloak to protect
from infection

wand to direct
patients (voice
difficult to hear
through mask)

Consult your physician at the first sign of symptoms.

Now We Know

- The techniques above were widely used but not effective.
- Antibiotics can cure the plague if started within 15 hours of the first appearance of symptoms. Streptomycin is the preferred drug, but gentamicin, tetracyclines, and chloramphenicol are also effective. Penicillin is useless against the plague.
- Bubonic plague bacterium is usually transmitted by fleas that have fed on the blood of infected rodents, most commonly rats. The bacteria multiply in the flea's upper digestive tract and eventually block it. When the flea feeds again, the block causes the freshly ingested blood to be regurgitated back into the bite, along with plague bacteria. The circulatory system of the bitten individual then carries the bacteria throughout the body, causing infection.

How to Avoid Rats

✪ Seal holes.

A rat can crawl through a hole 1 inch in diameter. Seal all visible holes and cracks in your home with mortar or shove in tight-fitting stones. Place an iron plate, a thick metal rod, or blocks of stone on the floor at the foot of all doors to obstruct the gap.

✪ Protect your food.

Place all food items, including cooking oils, in glass or metal containers with lids. Do not use wood, which a rat can chew through easily. If a non-wood container is not available, place food in a burlap sack and hang it from the rafters using a thin piece of leather. Do not hang food from thick ropes, which rats can crawl down. Food can also be stored underground, but only in a hole completely lined with metal or stone.

⭐ Dispose of waste promptly.
Do not leave food or human waste in the house at any time. Clean up spills immediately, before odors are absorbed into the floor.

⭐ Stay vigilant.
Rats are nocturnal, with peak activity at dusk and just before dawn. Assign each member of the family a three-hour "rat watching" shift during the night. If scratching is audible, scare the rats away or kill them using a shovel or other heavy implement.

Be Aware

Never touch a rat, even a dead one. Use a shovel to scoop up the carcass, then dispose of it away from your house. Scrub the area where the rat was found with soap and water, then treat with lye.

Nota Bene

From 1347 through 1350, the Black Death killed an estimated 25 million people—one-quarter of Europe's population at the time. Worldwide, the bubonic plague was responsible for 137 million deaths by the end of the 1700s. Outbreaks, though small, still occur.

JOAN OF ARC, 18, BURNED AT STAKE

Though Joan of Arc professed her devout faith in the Catholic church to her last breath, she was burned at the stake in 1431 for heresy. Just the year before, at the age of 17, Joan had led the French to victory against the English in the battle of Orleans, claiming to be inspired by the words of God. She played an active part in convincing the would-be French king Charles VII to step up to the throne that was rightfully his, and in the process she became a French national hero. Just a year later, in 1430, Joan was captured by English sympathizers and turned over to the English for 10,000 francs. In a trial based in partisan politics, she was convicted of heresy and ordered to be executed. Joan cried out for the saints as she burned alive, so fervent in her faith that afterward the executioner feared for his soul for burning a "saint." The executioner was correct: In 1456, she was posthumously retried and declared innocent of the heresy charges, and in 1920, Pope Benedict XV canonized her a saint.

History Lesson: History is the final judge.

Worst Jobs in Medieval England		
	Duties	Purpose
Leech Collector	Walk by riverbed to attract leeches on bare legs	Provide leeches for medical treatments
Fuller	Walk through vats of urine and wool fabric	Make stronger, softer cloth
Purple Maker	Smash mollusks in vat, add water and ash, and supervise pungent fermentation	Create purple dye for royal clothing
Arming Squire	Run into combat to replace broken armor on knights; clean knight's armor with sand, vinegar, and urine	Keep knights fierce, looking good

CHAPTER 4
THE RENAISSANCE: 1350–1600

THE COFFEE
KICKS IN

THE RENAISSANCE

1376   Zheng-He castrated by Chinese army; becomes one of the
        most successful admirals in Chinese naval history

1391   Toilet paper invented in China; first used by emperor

1453   Constantinople falls, renamed Istanbul; Greco-Roman
        civilization ends

1453   Turks introduce soap to the West

1455   War of the Roses begins in England

1468   Johannes Gutenberg, inventor of the printing press,
        dies impoverished

1478   Spanish Inquisition begins with search for heretics, Jews

1484   Spanish Inquisition expands to include search for witches

1487   Aztec King Ahuizotl assumes throne; sacrifices 20,000
        captives to celebrate

1492   Columbus arrives in America

1494   Medici expelled from Florence; fanatic Savonarola
        takes control

1495   Hundred-year syphilis epidemic begins in Europe; victims
        include Pope Julius II, Cardinal Wolsey, and Henry VIII

1509   Fungus and salt efflorescence damage first completed panel
        of Sistine Chapel ceiling

1512   Niccolo Machiavelli tortured and imprisoned for conspiracy

1519   Leonardo da Vinci dies

1523   Martin Luther smuggles 12 nuns out of convent in empty herring barrels; later marries one of them

1527   Holy Roman Emperor Charles V leads sack of Rome; artwork destroyed

1527   Left arm of Michelangelo's *David* broken during Florentine uprising against Medici

1531   Henry VIII separates from first wife, Catherine of Aragon

1536   Henry VIII's second wife, Anne Boleyn, beheaded

1537   Henry VIII's third wife, Jane Seymour, dies in childbirth

1540   Henry VIII divorces fourth wife, Anne of Cleves

1542   Henry VIII's fifth wife, Catherine Howard, beheaded

1547   Henry VIII dies, survived by sixth wife, Catherine Parr

1553   Michael Servetus, discoverer of pulmonary blood circulation, burned at the stake for heresy

1554   Princess Elizabeth of England imprisoned in Tower of London by half-sister Queen "Bloody Mary"

1556   Earthquake kills 830,000 in northern China

1560   Elizabeth Bathory, serial murderer responsible for deaths of 600 Hungarian girls, born

1564   The Council of Trent orders the artist Daniele da Volterra to add pants to some nude figures in Michelangelo's *The Last Judgment*

HOW TO PROVE
YOU'RE NOT A WITCH

1   **Get rid of any pets.**
Witches use animals as agents to carry out the devil's commands, so any animals in your charge, including any insects that enter the courtroom during your trial, may be interpreted as your "familiars" and offered by prosecutors as further proof of your status as a witch.

2   **Weep.**
Witches are unable to shed tears, so cry when you are arrested.

3   **React to pain during the needle ordeal.**
All witches have a devil's mark somewhere on their bodies to show that they have made a pact with Satan. During the needle test, any blemish, wart, scar, mole, or other imperfection will be poked to test your reaction. It is believed that the devil's mark is immune to pain and cannot bleed, so wince and cry out as each blemish is pricked.

4   **Sink during the water ordeal.**
Witches float in water because they weigh less than ordinary people. During the water ordeal, you will be tied at the hands and feet and thrown into a body of water in the presence of the court and members of the public. When your body hits the water, tense all of your muscles and imagine that you are made of lead or

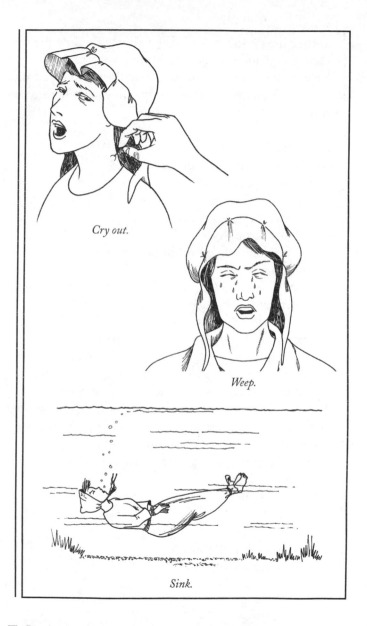

Cry out.

Weep.

Sink.

another heavy substance. Take short, shallow breaths before going under rather than filling your lungs with air. The guards will judge your ability to float, and if you sink to the bottom, they will probably pull you up before you drown.

Be Aware

- You are a witch if you have:
  - made a pact with the devil
  - had sex with the devil
  - practiced harmful magic
  - flown through the air
  - communicated with "familiar spirits" in the form of animals
  - murdered children to eat them or to make ointment from their rendered fat
  - met with other witches
- Because witchcraft is a *crimen exceptum*—an exceptional crime, on the same level as treason, conspiracy, forgery, and robbery with murder—the courts suspend normal rules of evidence to ease conviction.
- Unless you are a child or pregnant, any circumstantial evidence will lead to your torture in order to force a confession. Such evidence can include:
  - being named a witch by another witch testifying under torture
  - being a relative of someone executed for witchcraft
  - being homeless
  - committing adultery
  - learning too quickly

- making threats against another person that have come true
- being in the fields shortly before a hail shower
- making a sick person well
- attending church services sporadically
- attending church services regularly
- showing fear during arrest
- remaining calm during arrest
- If you are found guilty of witchcraft, you will be burned alive or hanged. In some regions, you will be strangled before your body is burned as an act of mercy.

Nota Bene

Witch hunts were most common in Europe from 1580 to 1630. More than 110,000 people were tried as witches, and 60,000 of them were convicted and put to death. About three-quarters of those convicted of witchcraft were women.

TOMAS DE TORQUEMADA

Head of Spanish Inquisition

BEST KNOWN FOR: Overseeing expulsion of Jews from Spain • Torturing heretics • Personally presiding over the burning of more than 2,000 Jews and other heretics • Sanctioning the murder of 30,000 Jews

BORN: 1420, in Torquemada, Spain

FAMILY: Grandmother a converted Jew; nephew of cardinal Juan de Torquemada

PHYSICAL DESCRIPTION: Stocky, with a bulbous nose and bushy eyebrows

EDUCATION: Dominican monasteries, studying theology at the Dominican convent of San Pablo in Valladolid

FIRST JOB: Prior of the monastery of Santa Cruz at Segovia

LEAST KNOWN FOR: Being part Jewish; kept a "unicorn's horn" near his plate as an antidote should he be poisoned

QUOTE: When Spanish Jews offered a tribute of 30,000 ducats if King Ferdinand would leave them in peace, Torquemada held aloft a crucifix and declaimed "Judas Iscariot sold Christ for 30 pieces of silver; Your Highness is about to sell him for 30,000 ducats."

DEATH: Despite a growing paranoia about being poisoned, he died of natural causes in 1498.

THE SEVEN HABITS OF HIGHLY EFFECTIVE INQUISITORS

1. Stretching the victim on "the rack" until his joints come apart.

2. Tying the prisoner's hands behind his back, hoisting him by the wrists, letting him drop several feet, and stopping him with a jerk before he reaches the ground.

3. Using "the pear," a segmented device forced into the victim's bodily openings and then expanded to the maximum aperture.

4. Forcing the prisoner to drink 30 pints of water.

5. Braiding the victim's limbs through the spokes of a wheel, then spinning it.

6. Slowly roasting the victim in a huge metal bull-shaped oven.

7. Disembowelment.

Nota Bene

Just 30 years after Gutenberg unveiled his invention, 122 towns in western Europe had printing presses, and by 1500 there were more than 1,000. This explosion of cheap, printed materials enabled Martin Luther to spread his ideas for church reform all over Europe in a matter of weeks, igniting the Protestant Reformation.

BYZANTINES DEFEATED BY OTTOMANS AT CONSTANTINOPLE

In 1452, Byzantine Emperor Constantine XI was anticipating a siege on Constantinople from Ottoman sultan Mehmed II. Knowing this, a Hungarian weapons innovator named Urban pitched Constantine his latest idea: a giant cannon more powerful than any weapon the world had ever seen, which could prevent enemies from breaking into the city. Constantine's military advisors sent Urban away, refusing to pay his asking price. Rebuffed, Urban took the idea to Mehmed, who immediately paid Urban four times the amount he'd asked for. Urban built a 26-foot-long cannon that could bury a cannonball 6 feet into the earth after traveling through the air for a mile—a record in size, power, and range. In March 1453, Mehmed and his army marched to Constantinople with the giant cannon on a cart pulled by 60 oxen. The siege began in April. The Byzantines did all they could do to stop the Ottoman artillery—they hung bales of hay and sheets of leather on the walls of the city to soften the blows of the cannonballs, but their defense did no good. After six arduous weeks, Constantinople fell to the Ottomans, due in large part to the strength of Mehmed's cannons. Constantine XI died in battle, and the Byzantine empire was effectively destroyed.

History Lesson: Invest in new technology—if you don't, your enemies will.

UNDER NEW OWNERSHIP

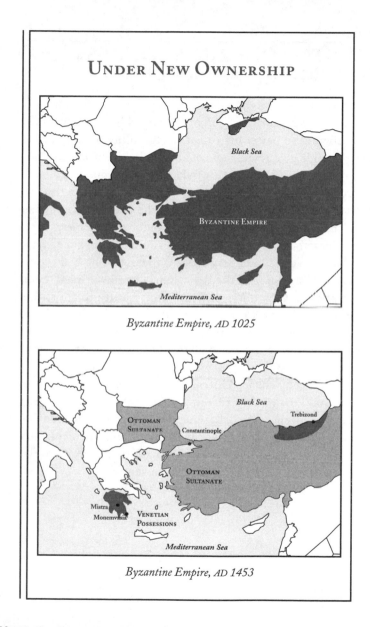

Byzantine Empire, AD 1025

Byzantine Empire, AD 1453

INVENTOR OF PRINTING PRESS CHEATED OUT OF SUCCESS

Johannes Gutenberg was an aspiring entrepreneur with poor business acumen and a mounting debt. In the 1430s, he developed several schemes to better his finances, stumbling on an idea for creating durable metal type that could accurately reproduce letters time and again. His innovation would allow 500 copies of a book to be produced in a single week—a vast improvement on the two months it took to copy a book by hand, the standard European practice at the time. To build his presses and make the metal type, he took a loan the equivalent of a million dollars from a merchant named Johann Fust. Gutenberg's idea worked, and he had orders for his entire first edition of the Bible even before he printed them. However, before Gutenberg had the opportunity to finish his printing and make back the investment, Fust called in his loan. When Gutenberg couldn't pay, Fust took him to court, and Gutenberg was forced to give up all the Bibles he'd printed, one of his two presses, and the expensive metal type he'd created, effectively removing any chance Gutenberg would have to profit from his invention. Fust made a fortune on Gutenberg's work, while Gutenberg fell deeper into debt. Gutenberg lived out the remainder of his days as a ward of the archbishop of Mainz, dying in 1468 a relative pauper. It wasn't until after his death that he received the credit he deserved for his world-altering invention.

History Lesson: Beware of unscrupulous lenders.

HOW TO NAVIGATE BY THE SUN

1 Set sail at high noon.
The sun will be directly overhead.

2 Stand near the mainmast of the ship.
The ship pitches and rolls the least at the mainmast, increasing the accuracy of your measurement.

3 Measure the altitude of the sun.
Crouch low to the deck and hold a mariner's astrolabe by its ring with the second finger of your right hand. Note the angle of the shadows cast by the sun, then turn the astrolabe to face the sun directly. Rotate the movable arm (the alidade) until the sun's rays pass through both the holes (pinnules) in the alidade, observing the point of light as it strikes the deck in front of you. The number on the astrolabe's scale indicated by the alidade's pointer is the angle of the sun's altitude. Do not suspend the alidade above your head and look into the sun to take the reading, as the position is unsteady and the light will be blinding, yielding an inaccurate reading.

4 Determine the angle of declination of the sun.
Declination is the angular distance between the sun and the earth's equator. Look at a declination table in your ship's almanac to find calculations based on the current date and appropriate year (leap year, or the first, second, or third year following a leap year).

horizon

level with horizon

Determine the sun's altitude by rotating the moveable arm on the astrolabe until the sun's rays pass through both its holes, then reading the number on the astrolabe's scale.

5 Determine the latitude of your home port.
Calculate the latitude with the following formula:
(90 degrees − altitude) + declination = latitude.

6 Sail to the latitude of your destination.
Using the astrolabe to determine your latitude as you go, sail north or south until you reach the latitude of your destination. Stay within sight of land or in known waters with favorable currents and winds for as long as possible.

7 Once you reach the proper latitude, sail east or west to your destination.
To return home, take readings with the astrolabe until you match your home port's latitude, then sail "down the latitude" east or west until you return.

Be Aware

- Any movement of the astrolabe during measurement will result in significant navigational errors.
- To produce accurate measurements, the astrolabe must have an alidade that fits snugly against the wheel, with perfectly aligned pinnules, straight pointers, and a precisely cut scale. Worn or corroded astrolabes should not be trusted.
- Because sailing across the latitude of one's home port is such a common practice, remain vigilant against pirates or ships from enemy nations as you return, as they can easily predict the route of your journey and lie in wait.

Now We Know

- Repeated use of an astrolabe—or a similar instrument called a cross-staff—to measure the sun's altitude often resulted in blindness. The back-staff, invented by John Davis in 1590, solved this problem by allowing the user to take measurements with his back to the sun. The sextant, which was invented in the eighteenth century, used colored glass filters to protect the user's eyes from harmful UV rays.

- Determining the exact position of a ship requires knowledge of longitude, which was impossible to determine at sea until the invention of the chronometer in the mid-1700s.

Nota Bene

Admiral Zheng-He (1371–1433) was China's greatest adventurer, far surpassing the skill of Western sailors of his time. He sailed his fleet of giant ships to more than 40 countries, traveling as far as East Africa and possibly sailing around the Cape of Good Hope.

SIZE OF ADMIRAL ZHENG-HE'S TREASURE SHIP VS. SIZE OF CHRISTOPHER COLUMBUS'S *SANTA MARIA*

Admiral Zheng-He's ship: 440 feet long, 186 feet beam (width), 9 masts, 12 sails

Columbus's Santa Maria: *75 feet long, 25 feet beam (width), 3 masts, 5 sails*

CONVERTED BY LIGHTNING

MARTIN LUTHER SURVIVES STORM, TAKES UP THEOLOGY

The electrical storm young Martin Luther encountered on his way home from law school in July 1505 changed the course of his life and, in turn, the course of European history. For his first 22 years, Luther had followed his father's wishes, pursuing an advanced degree in school and planning to enter civil service when he graduated. But on this fateful day, a massive thunderstorm roiled overhead, filling Luther with a feeling of intense dread. When a bolt of lightning struck close enough to knock him over, he cried out for help from Saint Anne, pledging to become a monk if his life was spared from the storm. He arrived home safely and made good on his promise— two weeks later he enrolled at a monastery, where he studied theology and ultimately created a new branch of Christianity.

History Lesson: The Lord works in mysterious ways.

POPE LEO X'S ARTISTIC PATRONAGE LEADS TO REFORMATION

When Giovanni de Medici was elected as Pope Leo X in 1513, the Catholic Church was facing unrest. A quick succession of Popes ensnared in corruption and personal scandal led to a weakening sense of the church's moral authority. But Leo, a member of the Florentine Medici family, was more interested in restoring Rome's cultural influence than in instituting church reform. Upon his election, Leo continued the Medici tradition of artistic patronage—he accelerated the construction of Saint Peter's Basilica, increased the holdings of the Vatican Library, and commissioned works from Raphael, Leonardo da Vinci, Michelangelo, and other celebrated artists of the day. All this grandeur cost money, so to raise funds Leo authorized a "jubilee sale" of indulgences, wherein believers could buy a more direct route to heaven. Though the practice of selling indulgences preceded him, under Leo's encouragement the sale of indulgences spread into Germany, where it incited the fury of theologian Martin Luther. In response, Luther wrote his Ninety-five Theses, outlining the church's need to reform the sale of indulgences and other abuses of power. Luther's writings quickly spread across Europe, sparking the Reformation movement and its far-reaching political, economic, and social effects.

History Lesson: Stick to your knitting.

HOW TO PAINT A CHAPEL CEILING

1 Commission a scaffolding.

To reach the ceiling, you will need to work on top of a scaffolding that spans the width and at least a partial length of the chapel. Keep the floor of the chapel clear for services by attaching the scaffolding at the walls, using wooden brackets to support arches that mimic the curve of the ceiling. Build bridges between the arches so you can access every part of the ceiling, and leave enough room at the top that you're able to stand with your arms above your head while painting. The scaffolding must be large enough and strong enough to hold you and your team of assistants, buckets of water, bags of sand and lime, and large rolls of paper. Suspend a layer of canvas beneath the scaffold to prevent spills and drips from hitting the floor.

2 Apply a fresh coat of coarse plaster.

Use a trowel to spread a 3/4-inch coat of *arriccio* (a mixture of slaked lime and sand) to the ceiling. This coarsely textured base coat will bond with a top layer of finer plaster, on which you will paint. If the ceiling has an existing fresco, chisel it off before applying the *arriccio*. The *arriccio* must dry completely before the painting can begin; this can take several months, depending on the dampness of the weather.

*Tie your paint pots to your waist and
work with a brush in each hand.*

3 As the *arriccio* dries, prepare cartoons.

A cartoon is a template for a figure or scene that will be traced onto the ceiling as a guideline.

4 Apply a layer of smooth plaster.

The fresco will be painted on *intonaco*, a smooth paste made from lime and sand that provides a porous surface for the pigments to adhere to. The damp *intonaco* absorbs the colors and seals them in as it dries. Use a trowel to spread a 1/2-inch layer of *intonaco* only in the area you can complete in a single day's work, as the plaster will remain wet enough to absorb pigments for just 8 to 12 hours. Wipe the *intonaco* with a cloth wrapped around a handful of flax to smooth the trowel marks and roughen the surface so the paint will stick to it. Then rewipe the ceiling with a silk handkerchief to remove any loose grains of sand.

5 Transfer the cartoon to the wet *intonaco*.

Intricate areas such as faces and hands require a more time-consuming process called *spolvaro*. Prick the outline with thousands of little holes, then secure it to the ceiling by pushing it firmly but gently against the *intonaco* or affixing it with several tiny nails. Transfer the outline of the drawing to the ceiling by hitting, or "pouncing," it with a bag full of dark chalk or charcoal dust. While pouncing, wear a hat with a wide brim to keep chalk out of your eyes, and cover your mouth with a wet cloth, if necessary. For parts of the drawing requiring less explicit detail work, such as arms, legs, and clothing, trace the lines of the drawing with a stylus, leaving marks in the plaster underneath.

6 Dilute pigments with water.

For best results, use the finest pigments available. Because of the chemical process that occurs between the pigments and the *intonaco,* unlike other contemporary forms of painting, the pigments do not require binding agents like egg yolk, glue, or earwax.

7 Begin painting.

Because time is of the essence, tie your paint pots to your belt for easy access, and work with a brush in each hand for speed—one for dark paint, one for light. Fill your brushes with diluted pigment, then squeeze the bristles between your thumb and index finger to remove excess water. To build up color, apply multiple coats rather than a single heavy coat. Lean backward slightly and extend your arms upward, raising your brush above your head to apply paint. Rest your arms frequently by placing them at your sides, and rest your eyes by focusing on objects that are at least 20 feet away every 20 minutes.

8 Correct errors quickly.

If you notice an error in your work while the plaster is still wet, scrape it off, apply a fresh spot of *intonaco,* and resume your work. If you do not catch the problem until after the plaster has dried, you will have to chisel away the entire day's work and repaint the area from the beginning.

Be Aware

- Occupational hazards of painting ceilings include pain in the back, head, and eyes; falling from the scaffolding to the floor; and working with *arriccio,* which smells of rotten eggs.

- While working on a fresco, the temperature cannot drop below 32°F; if the ceiling freezes, the color will easily flake off.

- The pigments in frescoes can blister and flake when an efflorescence of salt forms on the surface during damp weather. The efflorescence—calcium nitrate, also known as wall or lime saltpeter—appears when the plaster is applied too wet or when salts in rain-water leach through the plaster and onto the surface of the walls or ceiling.

- The palette a fresco artist can use is limited because many mineral-based bright colors cannot hold up to the corrosive lime in the *intonaco.* Some pigments change color due to chemical reactions with the lime, most notably azurite (blue), which turns green, and lead white, which turns black.

- Do not mix pigments with fixatives to paint on dry plaster. This technique may allow you to work with a wider range of colors, but sections painted while dry are prone to molds and mildews that grow on the binding agents used to mix the pigments. These are the first sections to decompose.

Nota Bene

Contrary to common belief, Michelangelo did not fresco
the ceiling of the Sistine Chapel while lying on his back.
This misunderstanding probably comes from a biography
of Michelangelo written by Paolo Giovio in 1527,
in which he described Michelangelo's technique as
resupinus, meaning "bent backward"—a word frequently
translated incorrectly as "on his back."

———

Michelangelo developed a rare form of eyestrain while
working on the chapel. Because he spent so much time
with his eyes focused upward, after several months' time
he could only read letters or study drawings when he held
them above his head at arm's length.

PRINCE VLAD III DRACULA

"Vlad Tepes," or Vlad the Impaler

BEST KNOWN FOR: Impaling, decapitating, gouging out eyes, skinning alive, boiling, dismembering, and physically disfiguring 40,000 to 100,000 people during his reign, including subjects he deemed poor, lazy, ill, or to be suffering from a physical impairment • Throwing garden parties next to freshly impaled victims

BORN: 1431, in the fortress of Sighisoara, Romania

FAMILY: His father, Vlad Dracul, was made prince of Wallachia (one of the three Romanian provinces) after murdering the ruling prince in 1437. In 1442, his father gave Vlad and his brother Radu as hostages to the Turks to prove his loyalty. Father murdered in 1447; younger brother Radu successfully led an army against him in 1462 and stole Vlad's kingdom. Vlad's first wife committed suicide as Radu's army approached. He later married a member of the Hungarian royal family.

PHYSICAL DESCRIPTION: Swarthy, with long, dark braided hair and a regal nose that hung over his long mustache

EDUCATION: Home schooled; later trained as a knight's apprentice

LEAST KNOWN FOR: Unifying his country and resisting the rule of foreigners

QUOTE: "I did this so no one would be poor in my realm."

DEATH: 1476, killed on the battlefield fighting against the Turks

HENRY VIII STARTS CHURCH OF ENGLAND TO MARRY AGAIN

In 1527, England's Henry VIII was in a bind. His wife, Catherine of Aragon, was getting older, losing her looks, and hadn't been able to bear a healthy male heir. Meanwhile, Anne Boleyn, a young woman of the court, was more than willing to try to bear Henry a son. To legally divorce Catherine and marry Anne, Henry needed a dispensation from the Pope, which the Vatican refused. A previous Pope had granted Henry special permission to marry Catherine, his brother's widow, 25 years earlier, and Henry was now asking him to claim that the church had been wrong in doing so. After six years of pressing for a sanctioned annulment, Henry cut ties with the Vatican altogether and created a new Church of England, freeing himself from the Pope's rule. In January 1533, Henry married Anne, and in May, his new church formally annulled his marriage to Catherine. Henry's Church of England fared far better than his marriage to Anne. When she, too, was unable to produce a male heir, Henry had her imprisoned in the Tower of London and eventually beheaded.

History Lesson: Choose your spouse carefully.

NOTABLE MONIKERS OF EUROPEAN RULERS

Most Fearsome	Least Fearsome
Vlad the Impaler	Ivar the Boneless
Charles the Hammer	Radu the Handsome
Peter the Cruel	Philip the Good
Ivan the Terrible	Ivan the Great
John the Fearless	Louis the Pious
Richard the Lionhearted	Theodoric the Great

HOW TO ESCAPE FROM THE TOWER OF LONDON

1 | Befriend your guard.
You will likely have one guard who is charged with tending to your cell. Offer the guard goods and coins brought to the prison by your visitors, or arrange to have friends within the prison system do the same on your behalf. After you've established a relationship, you can bribe him to buy things for you from outside the prison and deliver messages to and from friends.

2 | Ask the guard to bring you oranges, a quill, and paper.
Do not ask for all of these at once; space out your requests to reduce his suspicion. Save some of the juice from the oranges in a jug or another container, and fashion shapes out of the orange peels to send to friends. Cut off a short piece from the pointed end of the quill and attach it to a stick to create a makeshift pen. Then make a toothpick with the rest of the quill and leave it out so your jailer will see it. Tell the guard you plan to use the paper to wrap your orange-peel shapes so you can prove to friends that you're still alive and well.

3 | Communicate through invisible messages.
Use the orange juice and quill pen to create hidden messages on the paper, then wrap the dried orange peel shapes with the paper and ask the guard to deliver the packages to your friends. When your friends hold the paper to a flame, your words will appear.

Keep your body as close to the rope as possible.

4 | Befriend a prisoner in Cradle Tower.
Have your friends on the outside find out who is imprisoned in Cradle Tower, a short tower in the southeast corner of the outer curtain of the fortress. Befriend the prisoner by sending messages through your guard. The moat is at its narrowest at Cradle Tower, with just 30 feet between the tower wall and the wall separating the moat from the wharf. Cradle Tower also has a roof that is accessible from the prisoners' rooms, so you will be able to make your escape from there.

5 | Ask a trusted friend on the outside to assist in your escape.
Write a letter in orange juice instructing your friend to arrive in a boat on the wharf opposite the Cradle Tower on a specific night. Tell him to bring along a large, sturdy stake and a long, strong rope. Once he arrives, you will throw down a length of string tied to something heavy; he should tie one end of the rope to the string so you can pull it up into the tower with you.

6 | Convince the guard to allow you to visit your friend in Cradle Tower.
On the night of your planned escape, tell the jailor that you want to share a meal with your friend, and that he, too, can participate in the feast. Schedule and extend the meal so that it cuts into your guard's off-duty time. He will then be forced to leave you there overnight, as taking you across the garden at that late hour would provoke the sentries' attention and jeopardize his job.

7 Climb onto the roof.
If the guard locked the door to the roof before leaving, loosen the stone around the bolt with knives or other sharp tools.

8 Get the rope.
Tie one end of a long string to something heavy enough that your friend will hear it land on the wharf in the dark. Throw the object to him, keeping the other end of the string tied to your wrist. Once he's tied the string to one end of the rope, pull the rope to you.

9 Secure the rope to something strong.
Tie the rope around one of the cannons on the top of the tower. Make sure the rope line is taut between the tower and the ground.

10 Shinny down to the ground.
The tower is not much taller than the wall separating the moat from the wharf on the other side, so you'll have to work your way across the rope rather than just sliding down it. Position yourself so that you are hanging upside down with your stomach facing the rope and your head facing the wharf. Slightly extend one arm above your head and pull your lower body after you, with one leg locked over the other. Keep your face as close to the rope as possible. Continue in this fashion across the moat and over the wall to the wharf.

11 Cover your tracks.
Once your fellow escapee is across the moat, untie the rope from the stake. Cut part of it off so the rope hangs from the tower but does not stretch across the water.

12 Leave the country.
If you are caught, you and your co-conspirators will be executed.

Be Aware

- When communicating from prison, never mention the people you're writing to by name; use generic pseudonyms like "friend," "boy," "man," or "woman," which will not implicate anyone if the letters are intercepted en route.

- Unlike messages written in lemon juice, which can be seen if the paper gets wet but will disappear as the paper dries again, orange juice will wash away in water; it can only be read if held to fire, and then the letters are permanently visible. Orange juice messages cannot be read illicitly in transit without the intended recipient's knowledge, providing them with an immediate opportunity to refuse to accept the letter or deny that it is meant for them.

Now We Know

The method of escape described above was executed successfully in April 1597 by Jesuit priest Father John Gerard.

ACTORS SAVE BARD'S WORK FROM OBLIVION

Shakespeare's plays would have been lost to history but for the efforts of John Hemminge and Henry Condell, two actors from Shakespeare's acting company. In the early 1600s, dramas were typically published only by plagiarists who either stole manuscripts or handwrote them during live performances, publishing versions of plays riddled with errors and omissions. Several of Shakespeare's plays had been published in this incomplete form, including *Hamlet, Titus Andronicus,* and *Romeo and Juliet,* which in its early printed form was half as long as the actual play. But seven years after Shakespeare's death in 1616, Hemminge and Condell published 36 of his plays in editions that mirrored Shakespeare's original intentions. The plays were published in 1623 in a collection called the *First Folio,* which remains the definitive source from which all Shakespeare works are still derived.

History Lesson: All's well that ends well.

WORST DISASTERS OF THE RENAISSANCE

Event	Year	Death Toll
Shaanxi Earthquake	1556	830,000
Russian Famine	1601–1604	500,000
Dutch Flood	1530	400,000
Moscow Fire	1570	200,000
Naples Earthquake	1456	35,000
Lisbon Earthquake	1531	30,000

ELIZABETH BATHORY
The Blood Countess

BEST KNOWN FOR: Torture, mutilation, and murder of more than 600 young women and girls so she could bathe in their blood to bring back her lost youth

BORN: 1560, in Hungary

FAMILY: Well-connected member of the aristocracy—niece of the king of Poland and cousin of the Prince of Transylvania. Married Count Ferencz Nadasdy, known as Hungary's "Black Hero" for his bravery in fighting against the Turks. Had three daughters and a son.

PHYSICAL DESCRIPTION: Tall and slender with a smooth, alabaster complexion; known for her long black hair and, in her youth, her beauty

EDUCATION: Highly educated; able to read and write in at least four languages

LEAST KNOWN FOR: Despite servants' confessions and the accounts from the few survivors of her horror chamber detailing the circumstances of their ordeals, court officials never formally sentenced her to death due to her family connections; instead, she was locked in her castle for the rest of her life.

PETS: Kept several cats; is said to have prayed to the deity Isten, the supreme commander of cats

DEATH: 1614. She died alone, having been imprisoned in her castle for four years.

LAND, HO!

THE EARLY MODERN WORLD

1500s   The Aztecs invent game of *ollamalitzli*, in which players put a rubber ball through a stone ring. The losers were beheaded

1503   Christopher Columbus beaches his sinking ships in St. Anne's Bay, Jamaica, and spends a year shipwrecked and marooned

1520   Spanish army carries smallpox virus to Mexico; resulting epidemic kills off half of Aztec population

1521   Spanish army conquers, plunders, and razes disease-ridden Aztec city of Tenochtitlán

1532   Spanish army captures Incan capital of Cuzco; vanquishes Incan Empire

1533   Ivan the Terrible born

1544   Rats first appear in North America

1545   Spanish army carries typhus bacteria to Cuba; resulting epidemic kills 250,000 natives

1550   Mt. St. Helens in present-day Washington state begins a nearly constant, century-long eruption

1559   Henry II of France dies after being struck in the head with a jousting lance

1560   Spanish army carries smallpox virus to Brazil; resulting epidemic kills millions of natives

1588   Spanish Armada defeated by British

1590 John White returns to English colony on Roanoke Island; finds all 116 colonists he'd left there gone without a trace

1605 The Gunpowder Plot, a plan by English Catholics to blow up Parliament, thwarted

1616 Catholic Church forbids Galileo from continuing his scientific work

1618 Thirty Years' War breaks out across central Europe

1620 Pilgrim ship *Speedwell* found unseaworthy, abandoned; all 102 pilgrims pile into *Mayflower* for Atlantic crossing

1631 Mumtaz Mahal, wife of Shah Jahan of India, dies; shah erects Taj Mahal in her memory

1633 Galileo Galilei convicted of heresy for teaching that the earth revolves around the sun

1642 Charles I of England attempts to arrest his opponents in House of Commons; English Civil War begins

1649 Rump Parliament finds Charles I guilty of treason; executes him and abolishes monarchy and House of Lords

1665 Plague epidemic in London

1666 Great Fire of London destroys four-fifths of the city

1667 Accademia del Cimento, Florentine academy fostering scientific experimentation in manner of Galileo, closes

1681 Dodo bird extinct

1692 Giles Corey pressed to death for refusing to answer to charges of witchcraft

1699 The king of Spain bans the production of wine in the Americas

EXPLORERS OF THE NEW WORLD

Name	Active	Represented
Christopher Columbus	1492–1504	Spain
Juan Ponce de Leon	1493–1521	Spain
Giovanni Caboto (John Cabot)	1496–1499	England
Vasco da Gama	1497–1503	Portugal
Amerigo Vespucci	1499–1502	Spain, Portugal
Ferdinand Magellan	1505–1521	Portugal, Spain
Jacques Cartier	1534–1542	France

"Discoveries"	Namesake	Death
Cuba, Haiti, Central America	Colombia	1506, in Valladolid, Spain, without the wealth and nobility he felt he deserved
Florida; settled Puerto Rico	Ponce, Puerto Rico	1521, in Cuba, after Seminole Indian shot him with an arrow in Florida
Canada	Cabot Strait	c. 1499 in unknown circumstances; may have been lost at sea
Opened sea route to India via Cape of Good Hope	N/A	1524, in Goa, India, as Portuguese viceroy
Northern tip of South America	The Americas	1512, in Seville, Spain, as chief navigator for the Commercial House for the West Indies
Sailed around South America; first navigator to cross Pacific Ocean from east to west	Strait of Magellan	1521, in Philippines, in fight with natives; his ships returned to Europe to complete circumnavigation of globe after his death
St. Lawrence River, Quebec	Mount Jacques Cartier	1557, in France, disappointed that Canada hadn't yielded his sought-after diamonds and gold

HOW TO SURVIVE WHEN THE SHIP RUNS OUT OF PROVISIONS

✪ Sail to land.

Finding land is the best option when provisions become dangerously low. Virtually any land animal is safe to eat if the flesh is thoroughly cooked or salted. Provided they can be spotted and shot, wild goats, pigs, cattle, penguins, and monkeys will be popular options among the crew. Avoid eating unidentifiable mushrooms or plants, as they may be poisonous.

✪ Ration.

Place the crew on half rations, particularly when the likelihood of sighting land is low or unknown. Move to quarter rations as necessary. Be prepared for poor morale among the crew and added stress as they adjust to the new measures, including less rum to drink.

✪ Collect rainwater.

Put buckets on deck to collect water during storms. Hang sails, tarpaulins, or mats from the rigging during the rain and wring them out into buckets.

✪ Catch fish.

Assign members of the crew to catch fish congregating under the ship or in its shadow.

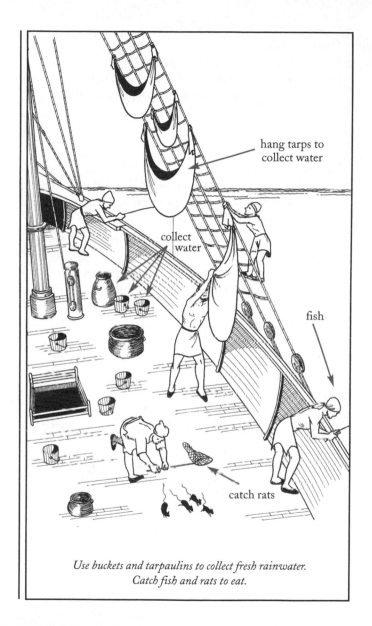

hang tarps to
collect water

collect
water

fish

catch rats

Use buckets and tarpaulins to collect fresh rainwater.
Catch fish and rats to eat.

★ Eat in the dark.
If any remaining grains on the ship are infested with worms or weevils, wait until nightfall to eat so as not to see the bugs in the food. Eating insect-ridden food is better than not eating at all.

★ Eat crumb dough.
Instruct the cook to sweep up bread crumbs from the bread room, mix them with water, and either bake this "dough" or serve it to the crew uncooked. (Peas and oats may be recovered in similar fashion from the hold.)

★ Hunt for rats.
Rats will be prevalent aboard the ship due to lax sanitary conditions. Catch them, gut and skin them, and roast them in the galley. Rats may also be traded among the crew for money or other provisions.

Be Aware
• The typical crewmember was allotted a ration totaling about 3,500 calories each day, with a diet of dried or salted beef or pork, salted fish, hard ship's biscuits, rice, dried peas, cheese, onions, garlic, oil, vinegar, water, and beer, wine, or other liquor.
• Ships' captains often chose to take less direct, island-hopping routes that would allow them to replace or restock rotting, insect- and rodent-infested provisions on board.

How to Treat Scurvy

⭐ Increase workload.
Physical activity aids in digestion and nutrition; scurvy can be brought on by laziness and sloth.

⭐ Bleed.
Scurvy causes an imbalance of the body's humors; bloodletting will restore equilibrium and dissipate the symptoms.

⭐ Drink ale fortified with pepper, cinnamon, ginger, saffron, watercress, and scurvy grass (spoonwort).

⭐ Eat deep-fried scurvy grass with eggs in train oil.
Train oil is the fatty scum at the surface of a pot of boiling seal carcasses.

⭐ Breathe the air of the land; bury yourself in soil.

⭐ Drink tea made from the bark and sap of an evergreen tree.
Take 10 to 12 branches from the tree and boil the bark and needles until the mixture is thick and the particles settle. Drink the tea every other day, and smear the dregs on the sores and ulcers on your legs. Recovery should occur within six days.

⭐ Drink three spoonfuls of lemon juice each morning.

Be Aware
• Symptoms of scurvy include loss of appetite; irritability; melancholy; weakness; diarrhea; fever; pain

and tenderness of the legs; swelling of legs and arms; thighs and lower legs covered with black blood spots; bleeding gums; blackening skin; ulcers; shortness of breath; semi-paralysis; swollen joints; muscle hardening; bluish purple, spongy gum tissue growing over teeth and immediately rotting; awful-smelling breath; teeth falling out; slow-healing or reopening of old sores; heightened sense of smell and hearing.

- Complete recovery from even advanced scurvy is possible if proper treatment is administered.

Now We Know

- Though the techniques described above were widely practiced, only the last two steps actually provided any relief from scurvy.
- Scurvy results from a combination of vitamin deficiencies, mainly vitamins C and B. It was occasionally compounded by an overdose of vitamin A from eating seals' livers. The vitamin deficiencies combined to break down the cellular structure of the body.
- Scurvy can be treated (and prevented) by taking daily doses of 250 mg of absorbic acid (vitamin C) and eating citrus fruits (oranges, lemons, limes, and grapefruits), berries, red and green bell peppers, tomatoes, and dark green, leafy vegetables. Symptoms will dissipate within one day to two weeks.

CORONADO FINDS GRAND CANYON, RIO GRANDE, BUT NO TREASURE

Francisco Vásquez de Coronado was determined to find treasures to rival those of the Incas and Aztecs in the unclaimed territory north of Spain's New World colonies. Rumors of the Seven Golden Cities of Cibola had been rampant in New Spain since about 1530, when an Indian named Tejo spoke of having visited cities filled with gold and silver as a boy. His story seemed to be confirmed when friar Marcos de Niza returned from an exploratory expedition claiming he had seen Cibola in the distance. In February 1540, Coronado and his army marched into present-day Arizona and New Mexico, arriving in Cibola five months later to find a small pueblo village without even a hint of wealth. Coronado ordered scouting parties that led to the discoveries of the Grand Canyon and the Rio Grande—but still no gold. Coronado refused to give up, trusting a dubious native he referred to as "the Turk" who promised treasure in a territory named Quivira. After wandering through Texas for 35 days, Coronado learned that the Turk was purposely leading them in the wrong direction. He enlisted a new guide and left most of his army behind in Texas, heading north into the plains of present-day Oklahoma and Kansas. When he arrived in Quivira, he learned that he'd been fooled yet again, as not even an ounce of gold was anywhere to be found. Despite expending such effort and claiming southwestern North America for Spain, without the gold, Coronado was considered a failure by the viceroy of New Spain.

History Lesson: Don't believe everything you hear.

AZTECS EMBRACE SPANISH INVADERS

In 1519, Aztec ruler Montezuma II welcomed the Spanish conquistador Cortez to his capital city of Tenochtitlán with gifts of gold, women, and food. Montezuma believed that Cortez was Quetzalcoatl, the fair-skinned, bearded god of fertility and the arts, who vowed to return to Tenochtitlán during a one-reed year—the first year of the Aztec's 52-year calendar cycle. In 1519, a one-reed year, the fair-skinned, bearded Cortez and his army landed and made their way inland toward the capital. At Montezuma's behest, the Aztecs put up no resistance. For a week after their arrival, the Spaniards toured the city as guests of the emperor, until they ultimately took him as a captive, removed him from his palace, and assumed control of the entire Aztec empire.
History Lesson: Don't be fooled by a pretty face.

WHO HAD IT WORSE?

	Mary, Queen of Scots	Montezuma
Title	Queen of the Scots, Queen of France	Ruler of Tenochtitlán
Lineage	Parents: Mary of Guise, a French noblewoman, and James V of Scotland	Uncle: Auítzotl, the eighth Aztec ruler
Age at Coronation	1	36
First Sign of Trouble	Husband found strangled; Mary implicated in plot	Mistakes Cortez as god; allows for city's capture
Backstabber	Queen Elizabeth I	Cortez
In Prison	19 years	7 months
Death	Accused of plot to kill Elizabeth; beheaded	Stoned by his own people, then stabbed by Cortez and his men
Legacy	Martyr, traitor	Oversaw demise of Aztecs

IVAN THE TERRIBLE
First Czar of Russia

BEST KNOWN FOR: Creating the Oprichniki, Russia's first secret police • Ordering executions meant to mimic the tortures of hell • The massacre at Novgorod, in which he sealed off the town and tortured and murdered the town's inhabitants

BORN: August 28, 1530, at Terem Palace in Moscow

FAMILY: Father, Russian grand prince Vasily III, died when Ivan was 3. Mother poisoned when he was 7. At 17, chose wife Anastasia from selection of virgins; she was poisoned 13 years later. Anastasia had six children; two survived infancy. In the 1570s, married five women in nine years. Murdered his son and heir, Ivan, in fit of rage.

PHYSICAL DESCRIPTION: Tall and powerful, with red hair and a long red beard. When angered, he foamed at the mouth.

EDUCATION: Educated by Russian nobility; considered one of Russia's more intellectual leaders

FIRST JOB: Proclaimed Grand Prince of Moscow at age 3

LEAST KNOWN FOR: After killing his son, pardoning many of those he had executed and paying for prayers to be said for their souls

QUOTE: "All of this has happened because of our sins and especially mine."

DEATH: March 18, 1584, while preparing for a game of chess. Buried in a monk's habit.

HOW TO DEFEAT THE SPANISH ARMADA

1 Assemble a large fleet of smaller ships.
The Spanish armada relies on its hulking galleons—40 warships with thick, heavy hulls and numerous powerful, short-ranged cannons. Though these ships are formidable, they are also slow-moving, with limited reaction time. Warships with smaller, thinner hulls, built for speed rather than for staying power, can outmaneuver the galleons in battle. Gain an additional advantage by amassing a fleet that outnumbers the Spanish galleons so you can gang up on the larger ships.

2 Employ long-range weapons.
The guns on the Spanish ships shoot heavy cannonballs capable of devastating any ship within their range, but they are difficult to load in the heat of a battle, and the cannons are only capable of throwing the shots a short distance. Equip your ships with long-barreled cannons that shoot smaller cannonballs a greater distance, allowing you to fight from farther away, out of range of the Spanish guns. These cannons have the added benefit of being faster and easier to load, allowing you to get off more shots more quickly.

3 Prevent the Spanish from picking up reinforcements.
Spain has the best-trained, most effective infantry in Europe. Their huge galleons, accompanied by dozens of support and supply ships, already carry tens of thousands of soldiers proficient at hand-to-hand combat. If

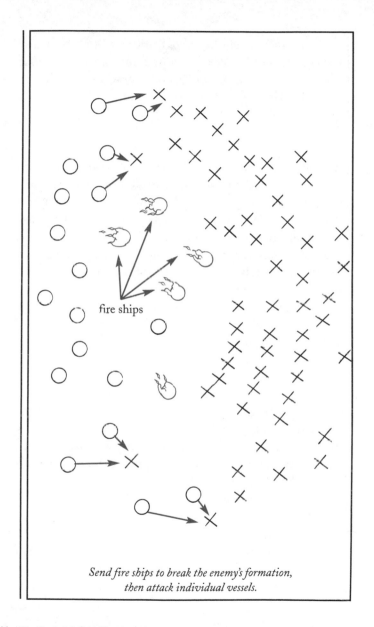

fire ships

Send fire ships to break the enemy's formation,
then attack individual vessels.

they are able to connect with more troops from the land, they will break past your fleet and invade your homeland. Block them from contacting armies in nearby territories under their control.

4 | **Launch fire ships to force the Spanish to break formation.**
The armada sails in a defensive crescent formation, making it impossible for your ships to approach any single warship without being destroyed by others nearby. To break up the formation, surprise the Spanish by discharging several fire ships into their midst. Fire ships are old vessels covered in combustible material such as tar, sulfur, pitch, and tallow that are lit on fire and blown into the enemy's formation by the wind. Wooden warships, with their sails and barrels of gunpowder, are highly flammable and can easily catch fire; the Spanish will be forced to break formation to sail away from the potential danger.

5 | **Attack lone ships during the confusion.**
Once the Spanish have scattered to flee the fire ships, overwhelm individual ships cut off from their allies by attacking each with several of your own swift, small, heavily armed boats. If necessary, board their ships and employ hand-to-hand combat to overtake the vessel and capture or destroy it.

6 | **Block convenient escape routes.**
After a successful battle, prevent any retreating Spanish ships from taking the fastest routes back to Spain by positioning your own fleet in the way. Force the armada

to sail home through unfamiliar territory to cause additional damage to their ships.

Nota Bene

In 1588, Spanish king Phillip II sent a large fleet of galleons manned by 19,000 soldiers up the English Channel to execute a plan to invade England. The English defended the channel with a fleet of small, highly maneuverable ships, engaging the Armada in two unsuccessful battles before they docked in the Spanish-controlled Netherlands to gather reinforcements. While the Spaniards waited for the arrival of additional troops by land, the English used the cover of darkness to send eight fire ships at them, forcing the Spaniards to break their crescent formation and allowing the English to take several of their ships. Afterward, the Spaniards opted to abort the mission, but the winds and the English fleet prevented them from traveling the familiar southern waters to Spain. They headed north, around the tip of Scotland, and the cold and treacherous seas around Ireland claimed even more of their ships. Only 60 of the 130 ships Spain sent to fight the English returned home safely.

FLOOD SAVES DUTCH CITY OF LEIDEN

In May 1573, early in the Dutch revolt against the absolutist rule of the Spanish king Phillip II, the Spanish army laid siege to the walled city of Leiden. The city had no troops and very little food, and therefore had to rely on the unconventional thinking of rebel leader Prince William of Orange, "William the Silent," for their liberation. On August 3, with the support of the patriots of Holland, William supervised the rupture of 16 dikes, and slowly the farms and villages of the low country surrounding Leiden filled with water. He recruited a fleet of 200 light-draught ships from the makeshift Dutch navy called the Sea Beggars, loaded them with weapons and provisions, and sent them over the flooded land to the desperate people of Leiden. By early September, the Sea Beggars had progressed to within five miles of the city walls, but to the dismay of Leiden's starving citizens, the Beggars' five-mile journey stretched on for a month. In addition to battling the Spanish for control of their forts, the Beggars faced retreating water that grounded their boats for several days at a time. Finally, on October 1 and 2, their luck changed when a gale reflooded the land. They mounted their final offense at the Spanish-held forts just yards from the city walls. Afraid of the ever-rising waters, the Spanish retreated overnight, and on October 3 the Dutch sailed into Leiden to distribute bread, cheese, and herring to citizens who had been forced to survive on rats, cats, dogs, and scraps of leather for two months. The Spanish troops never again forced their way into Holland, though the war between the Dutch and the Spanish, known as the Eighty Years' War, continued until 1648.

History Lesson: Don't get caught in a flood without a boat.

William the Silent, "Father of the Netherlands" and instigator of the Dutch revolt against the Spanish, was the first world leader to be assassinated with a hand gun. The Protestant prince was shot in 1584 by pistol-wielding, fanatical Catholic Balthasar Gerard, who murdered William to collect a 25,000-crown reward from Philip II of Spain.

24 AILMENTS CURED BY TOBACCO*

1. Cancer
2. Shortness of breath
3. Chest colds
4. "The grief of women" (labor pains)
5. Kidney stones
6. Scurvy
7. Stomachaches
8. Constipation
9. Toothaches
10. Arthritis
11. Abscesses
12. Worms
13. Boils
14. "Evil breathing at the mouths of children when they are overfilled with meat" (halitosis)
15. Venomous bites
16. Punctures from poison arrows
17. Cuts and wounds
18. Sores and infections, in humans
19. Sores and infections, in animals
20. Headaches
21. Cold sores
22. Hunger/starvation
23. Weariness/lethargy
24. Swelling due to exposure to cold

* According to Spanish doctor Nicholas Monardes, as published in his 1565 book *Two Books . . . about the Drugs from the West Indies used in Medicine,* translated into English in 1580 and published under the title *Joyfull Newes Out of the New Founde Worlde.*

PLAGUE EPIDEMIC SAVES ENGLISH GOVERNMENT

On May 20, 1604, five conspirators met in a London inn to hatch a plot: Blow up the Lords' Chamber during the upcoming state opening of Parliament—a ceremony involving King James I, his wife, Queen Anne, and all the leading government officials—to create enough confusion for Catholics to seize control of the country. But when a fierce outbreak of the plague reappeared in London that spring, the opening of Parliament was rescheduled for February 7, 1605. By January 1605, the plague had killed 37,000 of London's 210,000 citizens and had spread to the surrounding counties, causing yet another postponement, this time until October—and then again to November. These plague-induced delays cost the conspirators money, so with each passing month they recruited more people to their plot to help pay for rent and munitions. Finally, as the opening arrived, everything seemed to be going according to plan—the conspirators had filled a cellar below the Lords' Chamber at the Palace at Westminster with 36 barrels of gunpowder, five times the amount needed to decimate the chamber. But in the early morning hours of November 5, as conspirator Guy Fawkes lay in wait to light the fuse, the cellar was searched and the plot was thwarted. An anonymous letter, most likely sent by a late recruit, warned a member of the House of Lords, who immediately turned it over to the king. Fawkes and his co-conspirators were all killed, some while resisting arrest, others after imprisonment and trial. The failed plot increased anti-Catholic bias in England, and Catholics were forbidden to vote in Parliamentary elections until 1829.

History Lesson: The larger the conspiracy, the more likely it is to be uncovered.

HOW TO FORTIFY THE PERIMETER OF A NEWLY ESTABLISHED COLONY

1 Decide on the outer perimeter of the settlement.
The best way to protect your new development is with a tall, sturdy fence, or palisade, around the edges of the encampment to shield you from unfriendly natives, settlers from rival countries vying for the same land, and woodland creatures that will destroy your gardens and eat your crops. Decide on the safest spot for a gate and mark it out as such.

2 Chop down trees.
Find hardwood trees (oak, elm, cherry, ash, chestnut, red cedar) that are straight, 12 to 15 feet tall, and 8 to 10 inches wide. Use an ax to fell the trees, then drag them back to the settlement. The number of trees you'll need to complete the palisade will be determined by how large a space you are enclosing, but each 20-foot span will require about 25 trees.

3 Remove the trees' branches.
Using a saw, cut off all the trees' branches to create a straight log. Use an ax to hack the top of each tree into a point.

4 | Clear brush.
Remove grasses, trees, or underbrush growing in the area immediately surrounding the perimeter of the settlement. This will prevent your enemies from burning you out.

5 | Dig a trench along the perimeter.
Use a shovel to create a trench about 3 feet deep and 1 foot wide around the edge of the settlement. This is where the palisade will be constructed.

6 | Erect supports.
Starting at one corner of the settlement, stand one of the largest, sturdiest logs upright in the trench, with the pointed side facing up. Stand another strong log about 20 feet from the first. Connect the two upright logs by securing a 20-foot plank about 3/4 of the way between the two logs. Use a mallet to nail sharp wooden stakes the entire way through both the plank and each log.

7 | Add the fill.
Complete the gap between the two supports with more trees pressed as tightly together as possible. Use more spikes to secure the fill logs to the supporting plank.

8 | Fill the trench.
Push the dirt displaced by digging the trench back into the hole, along with some stones and other filling material. Tamp the fill into place around the logs. With the remaining dirt, make a 1- to 2-foot-tall mound at the bottom of the inside of the fence; forcefully tamp it to make it compact. The mound provides extra support for

Erect supports in the trench. Connect with cross planks.

*Press logs between the supports as closely together as possible.
Fill in the trench and tamp down the dirt to secure the logs.*

the wall while serving as a shooting platform on which you can stand to aim muskets and arrows through the top of the fence at attackers outside the fortification.

9 | Finish sealing the perimeter.
Repeat steps 6 through 8 until you have enclosed the camp except for the area with the gate. Station guards there to protect against invaders.

10 | Seal holes.
Fill in gaps between logs by pounding saplings into the holes. Leave any gaps above the horizontal support open so you are able to shoot from between them.

11 | Defend the fort.
The fort's walls will withstand arrows and small arms (but not cannonballs). However, the walls are vulnerable to scaling by attackers despite the pointed tips of the logs, so station soldiers around the fort to defend against invasion. Watch for arrows flying over the walls and down into the protected areas of the fort.

Be Aware
After the settlement becomes viable and you are ready to make it more permanent, you will want to reinforce the fence with buttresses to make it more secure. You may also consider adding bulwarks and artillery pieces at the corners of the camp for additional defense.

PILGRIMS LOW ON BEER, SETTLE AT PLYMOUTH ROCK

On November 9, 1622, after a 66-day, two-mile-per-hour journey across the Atlantic, the crew of the *Mayflower* had Cape Cod, Massachusetts, in their sights. By this time, due to delays encountered while leaving England, some of the passengers had been on the ship for four full months, and supplies were dwindling—especially the ever-important quantity of beer. In the seventeenth century, everyone, even children, drank as much as a quart of beer every day, as it was thought to be more pure than water. In sighting Cape Cod, the *Mayflower* was slightly off course—the passengers had been granted permission to settle in the colony of Virginia, which at that time extended as far north as the mouth of the Hudson River. Though the crew made one attempt to turn the ship south for their original destination, the ship encountered unfavorable winds, and the crew dropped anchor in Provincetown. The lack of provisions, coupled with the impending winter, led the passengers of the *Mayflower* to send expeditions into the surrounding areas rather than to head south again. By December 19, they decided they could afford to search no longer, and they agreed to establish their plantation at Plymouth.

History Lesson: Always make sure you have enough beer on hand.

FLOWER WORTH MORE THAN A HOUSE

The fortunes of thousands of amateur investors were ruined when the Dutch tulip market crashed in February 1637. From the early 1620s, tulip connoisseurs had steadily agreed to pay ever more extravagant prices for rare tulip bulbs, and when 3 bulbs were exchanged for a house in the summer of 1633, a financial bubble began. Prices steadily rose as more and more investors were drawn by the potential for quick money. Soon novice investors from nearly every social class were selling everything they had to join the fray. Bulb futures were traded at local stock markets, with notes changing hands multiple times a day as people entered contracts with the intention of instantly selling for a higher price. The market climaxed on February 5, 1637, when a family of orphans collected more than 90,000 guilders (almost $10 million in today's money) for a single bed of tulips planted by their recently deceased father. Within a week, the tulip market completely bottomed out. By May 1637, a bed of tulips worth 1,000 guilders in January could fetch only 6 guilders. Buyers and sellers went to court to settle differences over their now worthless claims. In May 1638, the government ordered sellers to cancel all contracts after buyers had fulfilled payment of 3.5 percent of the agreed price, leaving many in financial ruin.

History Lesson: Beware of investment frenzy: the bubble will burst.

TULIPOMANIA VS. DOT-COM BUBBLE

	Tulipomania	Dot-Com Bubble
When	1623–1637	1997–2001
Commodity	Tulip bulbs	Internet and tech stocks
Culprit	Tulip speculators	Venture capitalists, non-existent business models
Beginning	House traded for 3 tulip bulbs	Netscape shares increase from $28 to $58 despite company having no profits and little revenue
Peak	January 1637: Single bulb worth $1.06 million	March 10, 2000: Nasdaq composite index hits 5,048.62
Crash	February 3–10, 1637: Market disappears overnight	April 14, 2000: Nasdaq composite falls 9.67 percent in a single day
Low	May 1637: Tulips worth 1–5 percent of their value at peak	October 2002: Nasdaq composite bottoms out at 1,114.11, down 77.9 percent from peak

Nota Bene

Though it was not known at the time, during the tulipomania, the most popular varieties of tulips—the ones that changed hands for hundreds or even thousands of guilders—were actually infected with a virus that caused the intensity of the tulips' colors and the variations in the colors of their petals. A bulb that produced a single-colored flower one year might "break" (in other words, be afflicted with the virus) and produce a variegated flower the next. There was no way for speculators to know when this would happen, adding to the excitement over the potential payoff an investment may hold.

Value of One Viceroy Tulip Bulb at Height of Tulipomania

8 FAT PIGS + 4 FAT OXEN + 12 FAT SHEEP + 24 TUNS WHEAT +
240 guilders + 480 guilders + 120 guilders + 448 guilders +

48 TUNS RYE + 2 HOGSHEADS WINE + 4 TUNS BEER + 2 TUNS BUTTER +
558 guilders + 70 guilders + 32 guilders + 192 guilders +

1,000 LBS. CHEESE + 1 SILVER DRINKING CUP + 1 PACK CLOTHES + 1 BED +
120 guilders + 60 guilders + 80 guilders + 100 guilders +

1 SHIP   =   VICEROY TULIP BULB
500 guilders   *= 3,000 guilders*

ENGLISH LOSE NUTMEG CLAIM, GAIN BIG APPLE

Beginning in 1616, the English and the Dutch fought a series of naval battles over trade rights to the Spice Islands in the East Indies. Of particular interest was the English claim to Run, a tiny island thick with nutmeg trees. In the seventeenth century, nutmeg was as valuable as gold due to the commonly held belief in its curative powers. Dutch settlements in the Spice Islands outnumbered those of the English, and through force they were able to commandeer control of Run, too—but the English refused to back down. In 1664, King Charles II of England took revenge for Run and simply declared English ownership of the Dutch colony of New Netherland, present-day New York and New Jersey. Charles sought to unite the English colonies in New England with their holdings in the south to establish dominance over the eastern seaboard and expansion along the Hudson River. Charles gave the land to his brother, the Duke of York, who sent a small navy to attack the fort of New Amsterdam at the southern tip of Manhattan. The island was governed by the tyrannical Peter Stuyvesant, and the people of Manhattan felt no loyalty to him or the Dutch. Despite his orders, they refused to wage battle, and Stuyvesant was forced to surrender the island, along with the rest of New Netherland, without a fight. In 1667, the English and Dutch signed a treaty formalizing English acquisition of the colony now called New York and the Dutch claim to the island of Run. The Dutch lost their foothold in North America, never to regain power. **History Lesson:** If people don't fight, there won't be war.

HOW TO SURVIVE
WHEN MAROONED

★ Find drinkable water.

Gather rainwater by hollowing out the stumps of trees, but do not let the water sit for more than a day before drinking it. Tie rags around your ankles and walk through grass at dawn, then squeeze the dew from the rags into your mouth. The water in coconuts is safe to drink, though excessive consumption may cause diarrhea and dehydration. An island that appears to be dry may have a wet, mountainous interior, so move to higher ground to survey as much of the terrain as possible. In arctic environments, search for blue ice with round corners and that splinters easily—this is old sea ice and is nearly free of salt. Icebergs are also made of freshwater. If you are desperate, drink the water found in the eyes and spines of large fish.

★ Take care of your body.

Stay in the shade to protect yourself from the sun as well as from the reflection of the sun on the water. If you are in a tropical environment, dampen your clothes on the hottest part of the day to cool yourself and to avoid losing water through perspiration. If fresh water is readily available, use this water to moisten your clothes to avoid the boils and sores caused by saltwater. If you are in an arctic environment, find a cave or dig yourself a shelter in the snow to keep your body temperature up. Relax and sleep when possible.

Tie shirt securely around a forked branch.

Scoop fish from underneath to catch.

★ Find food.

Make a fish net by placing your shirt over a forked tree branch and tying off both ends. Pull fish out of shallow water as they swim over the net. Fish without spiny scales may be eaten raw or cooked. Kill seabirds by throwing rocks at them, as long as you have fire to cook them. You may be able to attract birds by flashing metal into the sky to get their attention. Do not eat anything if you are nauseated; drink only water and wait to eat until your stomach is calm.

★ Signal.

Make a signal fire by quickly rotating a small stick back and forth between your palms while one end is pressed against a piece of flat wood on the ground. The friction will create heat, which will ignite dry grass. Keep a small fire burning at all times, with plenty of fuel ready in case you spot a passing ship.

★ Keep a good lookout.

Chances are your ship was sailing on a known trade route, and other ships are likely to sail within several miles of your island. Move to high ground so you can see the horizon in every direction.

STANDOUTS OF THE GOLDEN AGE OF PIRACY

Samuel Bellamy

PIRATE NAME: Black Sam | SHIPS: *Sultana, Whydah*

DASTARDLY DEEDS: Took over mentor's ship; plundered 50 ships in just a few months; captured slaveship *Whydah* and made it his own

DEATH: 1717 shipwreck near Cape Cod

Sir Francis Drake

PIRATE NAME: The Dragon | SHIP: *The Golden Hind*

DASTARDLY DEEDS: Plundered Spanish treasure ships and colonies in New World; circumnavigated globe

DEATH: 1596 of fever, chasing Spanish holdings in West Indies

William Kidd

PIRATE NAME: Captain Kidd | SHIP: *Adventure Galley*

DASTARDLY DEEDS: Murdered his gunner, William Moore; captured Armenian ship *Quedagh Merchant*; actually buried his treasure

DEATH: 1701. Hanged by British; corpse dipped in tar and hung by River Thames as warning to other pirates

Bartholomew Roberts

PIRATE NAME: The Great Pirate Roberts | SHIP: *Royal Fortune*

DASTARDLY DEEDS: Raided 400 ships in four years

DEATH: 1722; shot in the throat during battle

Anne Cormac

PIRATE NAME: Anne Bonny | SHIP: *Calico Jack's Curlew*

DASTARDLY DEEDS: One of the few known female pirates; declared an "Enemy to the Crown of Great Britain" for raiding ships in the Caribbean

DEATH: Unknown. Captured by Jamaican authorities and sentenced to hang, she escaped death due to pregnancy

BLACKBEARD

Edward Thatch, Pirate of the High Seas

BEST KNOWN FOR: His terrifying appearance; he stuffed smoldering, slow-burning fuse cords under his hat to encircle his head with smoke • Seizing eight ships from the Charleston, South Carolina, port in one week • Removing the finger of a man who refused to give up his ring • Burning the ships and marooning the crews of those who resisted him

BORN: c. 1680, in Bristol, England

FAMILY: Married multiple times; had as many as 40 children

PHYSICAL DESCRIPTION: 6'5", 220 pounds, freakishly enormous at the time. His long black beard, which he braided into several pigtails, nearly covered his whole face, starting just under his bloodshot eyes.

FIRST JOB: Privateer based in Jamaica, plundering French and Spanish ships for Queen Anne during the War of the Spanish Succession.

LEAST KNOWN FOR: No evidence that he ever murdered anyone who wasn't already trying to kill him.

QUOTE: About the location of his treasure: "Nobody but the Devil and I knows where it is, and the longest liver shall have all."

DEATH: 1718. Killed near Ocracoke, North Carolina, by a soldier sent by the Governor of Virginia. Blackbeard's head was hung from the bow of the navy's ship as a warning to other pirates.

Pirate Articles on Board the Revenge

Every pirate on board Captain John Phillips's ship had to swear by the following code of conduct.

I. Every Man shall obey civil Command; the Captain shall have on full Share and a half in all Prizes; the Master, Carpenter, Boatswain, and Gunner shall have one Share and [a] quarter.

II. If any Man shall offer to run away, or keep any Secret from the Company, he shall be maroon'd with one Bottle of Powder, one Bottle of Water, one small Arm and Shot.

III. If any Man shall steal any Thing in the Company, or game to the Value of a Piece of Eight, he shall be maroon'd or shot.

IV. If at any Time we should meet at another Marooner (that is, Pyrate), that Man that shall sign his Articles without Consent of our Company shall suffer such Punishment as the Captain and Company shall think fit.

V. That Man that shall strike another whilst these Articles are in force, shall receive Moses's Law (that is, 40 stripes lacking one) on the bare Back.

VI. That Man that shall snap his Arms, or smoak Tobacco in the Hold, without Cap to his Pipe, or carry a Candle lighted without a Lanthorn, shall suffer the same Punishment as in the former Article.

VII. That Man that shall not keep his Arms clean, fit for an Engagement, or neglect his Business, shall be cut off from his Share, and suffer such other Punishment as the Captain and the Company shall think fit.

VIII. If any Man shall lose a Joint in Time of an Engagement, he shall have 400 Pieces of Eight, if a limb, 800.

IX. Man that offers to meddle with her, without her Consent, shall suffer present Death.

LET THEM EAT CAKE

THE ENLIGHTENMENT

1700 Tsunami hits Honshu Island, Japan, triggered by a 9.0-magnitude earthquake in California

1712 England taxes soap, a "frivolous luxury of the aristocracy"

1719 Daniel Defoe's *Robinson Crusoe* published

1725 Russian emperor Peter the Great dies

1730 German gun makers in Pennsylvania produce the Kentucky rifle, the most accurate rifle of its day

1740 **June:** Marquis de Sade born
      June: Frederick the Great awards first medal for combat bravery

1754 French and Indian War begins

1756 Seven Years' War begins; Austria and France ally against Prussia and England

1758 Maximilien F. M. I. de Robespierre, leader of the French "Reign of Terror," born

1759 French lose Quebec to English

1763 **July:** British forces distribute smallpox-infected blankets to Native Americans
      February: France loses Canadian colony to England at end of Seven Years' War

1765 Stamp Act meets with resistance in American colonies

1770 British soldiers fire into crowd of colonists in the Boston Massacre; five colonists killed and six wounded

1772	First partition of Poland by Russia, Prussia, and Austria
1775	Battles of Lexington and Concord begin American Revolution
1777–1778	2,000 American soldiers die at Washington's Valley Forge encampment over a harsh weather period of seven months
1778	**January:** English navigator Captain James Cook discovers the Hawaiian Islands, introduces venereal disease **May:** Voltaire and Rousseau die
1783	Lakagígar volcano in Iceland erupts for six months, building lava dam 40 miles long and 540 feet high
1787	Arthur Phillip sets sail for Botany Bay, Australia, with 11 ships full of criminals
1789	First tobacco advertisement in the U.S. **July:** Storming of the Bastille prison in Paris, symbolic start of French Revolution
1792	**April:** Tiradentes, leader in Brazil's fight for independence from Portuguese, drawn and quartered **April:** Highwayman Nicolas Jacques Pelletier first person under French law to be executed by guillotine
1793	King Louis XVI sentenced and guillotined
1795	General Napoleon Bonaparte leads rout of counterrevolutionaries in the streets of Paris, beginning his rise to power
1798	The first big U.S. bank robbery, at Philadelphia's Carpenter's Hall
1799	**November:** Napoleon overthrows the Directory and becomes first consul of France **December:** George Washington dies

HEROIC PETER RUINS HEALTH, THROWS RUSSIA INTO CHAOS

Peter the Great's desire to give his country a navy and a warm-water port helped make Russia into a nation to be reckoned with, but his obsession with the water ultimately left the nation vulnerable to disputes over succession. From a young age, Peter was fascinated with seafaring and shipbuilding, leading to his oversight of the creation of a respectable Russian navy during his reign. He led several successful military campaigns, extending Russia's landholdings to the Baltic Sea to gain more favorable trading conditions with western Europe. By 1724, Peter's exertion was catching up to him, though he was unable to admit to losing his physical strength. That November, while sailing through the stormy late-autumn waters of the Baltic, Peter spotted a ship full of soldiers who'd run aground on a sandbar. His heroic impulses, comfort with the sea, and love of the military overtook him, and he insisted on helping in their rescue. He jumped into the cold water and worked for several hours to push the boat from the shoal. Peter caught fever the next day, and though he continued to lead the country, he never fully recuperated. He died just four months later—before he'd made out a will stating who would take the throne after him. This lack of legitimate succession led to a power-grab known as Russia's "era of palace revolutions," which saw six rulers turn over in a short 37 years.

History Lesson: Stay focused and know your limitations.

ANIMALS EXTINCT BY 1800

DODO BIRD: *The flightless, 50-pound dodo bird lived on the island of Mauritius until its extinction in 1681.*

AUROCHS: *This wild ox once inhabited all of Europe and northern Africa; the last of the species died in central Poland in 1627.*

STELLER'S SEA COWS: *Slow moving creatures first seen in the Bering Sea in 1741. The species was extinct by 1768.*

THE SADDLE-BACKED RODRIGUES: *Giant turtles native to the island of Rodrigues in the south-western Indian Ocean were hunted to extinction by 1800.*

CHURCH REJECTS FRANKLIN'S LIGHTING ROD

When in 1752 Ben Franklin showed that a metal rod could safely send electricity into the ground and therefore protect a building from lightning, many Christian leaders were outraged. For centuries Christians believed that lightning was sent by God as a punishment for sins—and Franklin's redirection of this tool of God's wrath was seen as an affront to God's will. Though lightning rods were quickly put to use by the scientifically minded in the colonies and across Europe, churches, often the tallest and most vulnerable structures in towns and villages, were slow to adopt the new technology. Rather than erecting lightning rods, priests continued with the tradition of consecrating the bells that hung in church spires; during thunderstorms, the metal bells would be rung as special prayers to ward off the storm were recited below. In the 30 years in which German churches rejected Franklin's invention, 400 church towers were struck and 120 bell ringers were killed. But clergy were shown the most compelling reason for using the rods when lightning hit the church at Saint Nazaire in Brescia, Italy. As in many churches at the time, Saint Nazaire's underground vault was used to store gunpowder, and at the time of the storm it held more than 200,000 pounds of it. When lightning stuck, the church exploded, destroying one-sixth of the city and killing more than 3,000 people. After this, churches maintained their previous rituals to ward off the storms, but many also took the added precaution of installing Franklin's lightning rod as well, deciding that science and religion could work together to prevent destruction.

History Lesson: Don't be frightened of new ideas.

HOW TO WARN THE TOWN OF INVASION

⭐ Warn your leaders.

The invading forces are likely to target influential members of the insurgency to cause confusion and disrupt their plans. The first goal is to warn government representatives and militia leaders within striking distance of the amassing colonial forces that they are in danger.

⭐ Put signal warning system into action.

If the threat of invasion seems ever present, arrange a warning system that will alert all supporters and militia members in the area. Tell supporters that when an invasion is imminent, a signal light will be shone at the highest point in the town (typically this is the church belfry). If your city is vulnerable from both the river and the land light one lantern if the enemy is approaching by land, or two lanterns if the enemy is approaching by water. The lanterns should be fully oiled and high-wicked for added illumination.

⭐ Sneak past enemy guards.

If the city is under guard by the colonial forces and you must leave the city limits past curfew to reach the leaders, slip past the enemy guard posts at the edges of the city. A team member with friends in the colonial army is the best candidate for leaving the city on horseback—he can mingle with a friendly group of soldiers who are leaving town. Another team member can leave the city by water, rowing out of the city by boat under cover of darkness and finding a horse on the other side to continue with the journey.

★ **Alert patriots of the impending invasion.**
While traveling to warn leaders of the attack or to take your defensive position, quickly stop at the homes of other patriots. Urge them to take up arms and gather at the appropriate place to defend against the colonial troops. Ask them to pass the message on to others sympathetic to the cause.

★ **Work as part of a team.**
Assign a partner to duplicate your mission, whether activating warning systems or alerting leaders. Take different routes so that if one of you is captured the other will still have a chance of getting through.

★ **Be suspicious of fellow travelers.**
Pairs of men on horseback lurking by the side of the road may be soldiers sent there to support the invasion and thwart the warning system. The pair may be part of a more elaborate trap—there might be more officers hiding in trees or brush nearby.

★ **Elude pursuers on side roads.**
If chased by enemy soldiers, charge down side roads at full gallop. You should be able to outrun your pursuers, since they will be unfamiliar with the territory and uncomfortable with taking the dark roads at such a fast clip.

*Shine the signal light and ride to warn fellow patriots
of the impending invasion.*

Secure all munitions in the vicinity.

After the government representatives have been successfully cautioned, warn militia leaders to secure their weapons stashes so they are not confiscated by the advancing troops.

Nota Bene

Although Paul Revere usually takes all the historical credit for spreading the word of the British invasion, Israel Bissell, a 23-year-old post rider, was really the one who got the news out to the colonies. He traveled by horse for five days, from Boston all the way to Philadelphia, bearing a dispatch from General Joseph Palmer that has come to be known as "the Lexington Alarm." Bissell made stops in at least 17 towns on his journey, rousing the excitement of patriots anxious to fight for American rights all along the way. The letter sparked an armed revolt against the British in New York City, and in Philadelphia no fewer than 8,000 citizens were present for the public reading of the letter. The war for American independence had begun.

KING GEORGE PROVOKES COLONISTS' QUEST FOR INDEPENDENCE

Even after several battles between American colonists and British regulars outside Boston in 1775, the majority of America's colonists considered themselves proud Englishmen. Most of the soldiers in George Washington's army were fighting not for American independence, but for the colonies' representation in the British Parliament. But King George III, like most rulers of his day, was not interested in negotiating terms with subjects who'd taken up arms, especially when news of the 1,000 British casualties at the Battle of Bunker Hill reached London at the end of May. When Parliament reconvened in October, King George publicly accused the colonists of pursuing independence from England and announced that he was sending more soldiers—including a force of foreign mercenaries —to quash the rebellion. When copies of the king's speech arrived in the hands of colonial soldiers in January of 1776, his words did everything but put down the war. The colonists were so affronted by their king planning to bring foreign soldiers into what they had seen as an internal squabble that it spurred many of them into full-blown rebellion. Even formerly moderate colonists lost their desire for a diplomatic resolution, and for the first time thoughts of forming an independent nation became widespread throughout the colonies.

History Lesson: Pursue diplomatic options before escalating to war.

NOSTRUMS OF THE ENLIGHTENMENT

Product	Inventor	Claim
Dr. Bonker's Celebrated Egyptian Oil	Dr. Bonker	Cures skin infections and internal maladies
Perkins Patent Tractors (Brass and Iron Rods)	Elisha Perkins	Redirects body's electricity to cure ailments and infections
Morison's Vegetable Pills	James Morison	Cleanses blood and bowels, eradicates all diseases
Make-Man Tablets	Robert N. Harper	Cures tuberculosis, irritability, and "female disorders"

COLONIAL CHRISTMAS PRESENT

GENERAL WASHINGTON ROUTES HESSIANS IN TRENTON

By Christmas Day, 1776, General Washington led a beaten-down army of just 3,500 men. After four consecutive defeats, Washington's troops appeared so downtrodden that the commander of the Hessian mercenaries in Trenton, Colonel Johann Rall, didn't think them capable of mounting an effective attack. Despite receiving a warning late in the afternoon on December 25 that Washington was planning an attack, Colonel Rall went to a Christmas party. As Washington amassed 2,400 of his troops and made a daring nighttime crossing of the Delaware River, Rall received yet another warning. But since he was engaged in a card game, he stuffed the message—unread—into his pocket. At 8:00 A.M. on December 26, Washington's army made an attack on Trenton and within 45 minutes the Hessians surrendered. Colonel Rall was mortally wounded in the battle.

History Lesson: Don't underestimate your enemy.

HOW TO LEAD AN ARMY ACROSS A RIVER WITHOUT BEING NOTICED

1 | Cross at night or on a day with bad weather.
Though rain or snow will add time to the journey and make it more treacherous, it will also provide a cover of noise and increase the element of surprise.

2 | Keep the plan secret.
Tell only other generals and those few officers whose regiments would be integral in carrying out the plan that you are taking the army across the river.

3 | Acquire boats.
Order the seizure of all large, flat-bottomed boats or sloops in the area, particularly high-sided boats normally used for transporting freight. Destroy all remaining boats of any size 10 miles above and 10 below your position; this will prevent the enemy from using such craft for bringing in reinforcements.

4 | Choose crossing point.
Cross at least 10 miles below the enemy's last known position, at a narrow, smooth spot in the river that is not crowded with rocks.

5 | Prepare equipment.
Tell the troops to be "under arms, with packs and everything." Issue three days' rations to each man and give orders to keep blankets dry and at the ready.

6 | Ensure secrecy.
Dispatch sentries to guard a quarter-mile arc of land around the embankment where the army will cross. Assign a password for the army units, and instruct the sentries not to allow anyone who does not know the password to enter or leave the area surrounding the embankment. Put white paper into the officers' hats to distinguish them from the rest of the troops in the dark.

7 | Demand absolute silence.
Use rags to muffle wagon wheels or anything that might make noise. Forbid soldiers from talking or even coughing. Orders pass in whispers from officer to officer, and then to the troops.

8 | Assemble at the embankment.
When darkness falls, move the first regiment to the water. Assign strong experienced seamen to operate the boats.

9 | Cross the river.
Load as many men into the boats as possible, then instruct the seamen to use oars and poles quietly when moving the boats across the river. If the sides on the boats are high enough, have the men stand rather than sit to fit more on each boat at a time.

Crossing during a storm will provide an additional cover of noise to help maintain the element of surprise.

10 Send the boats back for more soldiers.
Do not transport artillery or horses until all troops have crossed safely.

11 Assemble men on the other side.
Continue to enforce the silence. Once all men, weapons, and horses have completed the crossing, lead the army to its destination.

Nota Bene

Washington had originally planned for 6,000 men to cross the Delaware and attack the British and Hessian troops stationed at Trenton. Because many men were ill, and several of Washington's subordinates ignored the general's orders, only about 2,400 troops made the famous crossing.

BENEDICT ARNOLD
Continental Army General

BEST KNOWN FOR: Betraying his country by revealing plans to invade Canada • Making plans to hand over West Point, New York, to the British in exchange for £20,000 (roughly $1 million today)

BORN: 1741, in Norwich, Connecticut

FAMILY: Second of six children. Once quite wealthy, his family suffered after Arnold's father failed in business. Married twice; had eight children. Met his second wife, boisterous socialite Peggy Shippen, when he was 38 and she was 18. Peggy introduced him to British major John Andre, with whom Arnold plotted his treachery.

PHYSICAL DESCRIPTION: A strong, burly man with a long, regal nose and deep-set eyes. Crippled after horse fell on his leg in battle

EDUCATION: Attended school at Canterbury until forced to withdraw due to his father's debt; apprenticed at cousins' apothecary business

FIRST JOB: Shopowner; sign read: "B. Arnold Druggist, Bookseller, &c. From London Sibi Totique" (for himself and for all)

LEAST KNOWN FOR: Heroic leadership of American troops in early years of the war; rallied for a victory at Saratoga, which convinced the French to fully support the Americans

QUOTE: "I have ever acted from a principle of love to my country . . . however it may appear inconsistent to the world, who very seldom judge right of any man's actions."

DEATH: 1801, in London, severely in debt

BLIGH'S MEN REVOLT AFTER TAHITIAN SABBATICAL

In late December 1787, Commanding Lieutenant William Bligh and the 45-man crew of the HMAV *Bounty* sailed for Tahiti to collect breadfruit plants that would be a cheap source of food for slaves on Caribbean plantations. The *Bounty* arrived at its destination during the wrong season for collecting breadfruit saplings, and Bligh and his men had to wait almost six months to complete their charge. While they were at port, Bligh was lax with discipline, allowing his men to go ashore and enjoy the island. By the time the *Bounty* set sail again in April, many of the men had developed relationships with Tahitian women and were loath to leave their tropical retreat. Taking orders from a hot-tempered captain—especially when Bligh had been lenient for so long—was now more than many of them could bear. After three weeks back at sea, Bligh's first mate and old friend, Christian Fletcher, led a mutiny against him. On the morning of April 28, Fletcher and his compatriots hauled Bligh to the deck in his nightshirt and set him adrift on a small boat with 18 of his loyal men. Fletcher turned the *Bounty* around and returned to Tahiti, and he and some of his crewmates settled nearby Pitcairn Island with several Tahitian women and men. Bligh and his sailors made an amazing 3,600-mile journey to the island of Timor in their 23-foot, open-air boat, subsisting for 48 days on food and water that would typically have lasted only five. When he returned to England, Bligh was promoted to captain and later to vice-admiral, eventually surviving mutinies on two more of his ships.

History Lesson: Spare the rod, spoil the crew.

HOW TO WIN A FIGHT WITH BAYONETS

★ Maintain eye contact with opponent.
Watch his weapon and body using peripheral vision.
Size up each moment of the fight, pursuing all openings
and weaknesses your opponent reveals.

★ Make constant, unpredictable movements.
Do not allow your opponent to take a clean shot or to
anticipate your next move.

★ Growl.
Make aggressive, threatening noises to frighten your
opponent and instill confidence in your own abilities to
finish the fight.

★ Start in the attack position.
Stand with your feet a comfortable distance apart, with
your body bent slightly forward at the waist, knees
slightly bent, and weight balanced on the balls of your
feet. Hold the musket firmly, with your dominant hand
on the butt or just behind the trigger guard and your
other hand on the grip below the barrel. Position the
musket diagonally across and slightly away from your
body at about nose level.

Thrust the bayonet.
Grasp the musket tightly and pull the butt in close to your hip; partially extend your nondominant arm, guiding the point of the bayonet toward your opponent's face, throat, abdomen, or groin. Step forward with one leg and push with the full power of your body's movement, using your back heel, waist, and hips rather than relying solely on upper body strength. Upon penetration, twist the bayonet. To withdraw, shift your weight back, and pull out along the line of penetration. Resume the attack position to continue with the fight.

Strike with the musket butt.
Step forward with the leg opposite your dominant hand and raise the musket in an arc, using your dominant hand to force the butt of the musket underneath your opponent's weapon or onto a vulnerable area of his body (anywhere from his face to his thighs). If delivered with enough force, a strike from the butt of the musket to a bony area can disable your opponent and possibly kill him. Resume the attack position.

Smash with the musket butt.
Push the butt of the rifle upward until it is horizontal, with the muzzle just above your nondominant shoulder and the bayonet pointing behind you. Step forward with the leg opposite your dominant hand and forcefully push with both arms, slamming the butt into your opponent's face. This move is often effective after striking with the musket butt.

Step forward with your leading foot.

Strike your opponent's musket.

Deflect the opponent's musket to your right.

★ **Parry your opponent's attacks.**
Counter the movements of your opponent by quickly raising your bayonet and striking the opponent's musket with your own. If the butt of his musket is at his left hip, deflect his thrust to your right; if the butt of his musket is at his right hip, deflect to your left. This will throw your opponent off balance and enable you to follow up with a thrust, strike, or smash.

★ **Block surprise attacks.**
To stop an opponent from striking your groin with the butt of his musket, extend your arms downward and slightly out from your body, catching his weapon at the center part of your musket. To stop a butt stroke to your upper body or head, hold your musket vertical so your opponent's weapon will hit at the center of your musket. Counterattack immediately.

★ **Be relentless.**
Quick action is imperative in a bayonet fight. You are fighting for your life.

Be Aware

• In the majority of bayonet charges, the defensive side flees before any contact is made. Bayonet charges are often more of a symbolic coup de grâce meant to finish off the morale of the opposition than an order to actually engage in hand-to-hand combat. Because soldiers running toward a line with bayonets drawn present such an intimidating sight, the commander with the field advantage often delivers the order to stop the battle by chasing the remaining enemy troops from the field. If you hear your field commander give the order for a bayonet charge, you can assume that you are on the winning side of an almost-finished fight.

- Most actual bayonet fights occur not on a battlefield but in close combat situations in villages, woods, or gardens or on highly irregular, broken terrain.
- Aiming at an opponent's breast may lead to impalement of the breastbone, making removal of the bayonet very difficult.

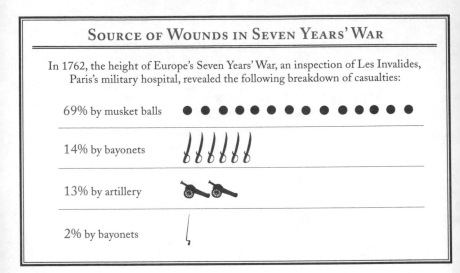

Source of Wounds in Seven Years' War

In 1762, the height of Europe's Seven Years' War, an inspection of Les Invalides, Paris's military hospital, revealed the following breakdown of casualties:

69% by musket balls

14% by bayonets

13% by artillery

2% by bayonets

Fashion Emergencies of the 1700s

Device	Purpose	Side Effects
Powdered Wig	Cover baldness	Smelled, especially in hot weather; fear that hair came from plague-ridden corpse
Wax Makeup	Hide smallpox and chickenpox scars	Standing too close to a fire would literally melt face off
Ceruse Makeup	Whiten complexion	Hair loss (especially eyebrows), impotence, sterility, kidney damage, tremors, high blood pressure, depression, insomnia, hearing loss, wrist drop, death
Foot Binding	Make feet 3 inches long	Toes curl under, arches of feet break; gangrenous toes; walking very difficult; forced to crawl or walk on knees around house
Belladonna (Deadly Nightshade) Drops	Dilate pupils for wide-eyed look	Blurry vision, increased heart rate, glaucoma, blindness

LOUIS XVI'S INVOLVEMENT IN AMERICA BRINGS DOWN FRENCH MONARCHY

In May 1778, France became America's official ally in the colonies' war for independence from Britain. In the next five years, France's king Louis XVI spent 1,066 million livres on America's war, with 997 million of that money raised from loans the monarchy had taken at a high rate of interest. In 1786, almost half the government's income was spent in paying back debt, and the monarchy was all but bankrupt. But when the king's finance minister proposed raising money by repealing the nobility's tax immunity, the aristocrats balked, forcing Louis to summon the Estates-General—elected representatives of each of the three "estates" of clergy, nobles, and commons—for the first time since 1614. That the king had to appeal to his subjects for approval of a proposed tax reform revealed the monarchy's vulnerability, and the commoners were quick to take advantage of the weakness. The meeting commenced in May 1789, and by June 27 the commoners of the Third Estate put Louis into a position where he had no choice but to approve the creation of a National Assembly to draw up a constitution, effectively eliminating his absolute power. Just a few weeks later, on June 14, a mob fed up with high prices and the repressive power of the monarchy stormed the Bastille prison in Paris, and the French Revolution had begun.

History Lesson: Don't spend beyond your means.

HOW TO BUILD A STREET BARRICADE

1 Build the barricades at strategic locations.
Block access to all major roads into the city, as well as important intersections and streets leading to the base of operations.

2 Requisition supplies from local merchants.
To avoid carrying supplies all over the city, visit local stores sympathetic to the cause and request sacks of plaster, wheelbarrows, spades, pickaxes, hammers, chisels, trowels, buckets, and troughs.

3 Remove paving stones from the street.
Paving stones are the main component in an effective barricade. A double-walled barricade, with each wall 10 feet tall and several feet wide, will require digging up 50 yards of the street, or about 9,200 paving stones.

4 Build the walls.
Use the tools acquired from the merchants to erect the walls of the barricade. Leave approximately 20 feet between the walls to provide room for the storage of weapons as well as space to assemble and fight the advancing army.

5 Arm the barricade.
Place a cannon or machine gun at the top of each wall.

Build barricades out of paving stones, doors, overturned carts, and other strong, heavy materials.

6 Construct "lateral barricades."

Cut through the inner walls of the first and topmost floors in the houses that line the blocked street. This will allow a means of escape from the street barricade, but it will also provide another rampart for fighting. Use unhinged doors or shelves from stores as shields by placing them over windows or balconies. Cut notch holes in the shields from which you can spy and shoot at the enemy army.

Be Aware

If you do not have time to construct a highly fortified barricade, any combination of the following items will work so long as the barrier is at least 6 feet tall and several feet wide: mattresses, sandbags, overturned vehicles, doors, street grates, grates from trees.

WHO HAD IT WORSE?

	Marie Antoinette	Napoleon Bonaparte
Title	Queen of France	Emperor of France
Nickname	Madame Deficit	Le Petit Caporal (The Little Corporal)
Presided Over	French Court	Newly formed French Empire
Age at Coronation	19	35
Years Married Without Children	8	15
Angered	French revolutionaries	Coalition including England, Russia, Spain, Portugal, and Prussia
Turn for the Worse	Accused of immoral relationship with cardinal	Winter retreat from Russia
Fatal Blow	Collapse of monarchy, 1792	Loss at Waterloo, 1815
Years in Captivity	2	6
Final Days	Solitary confinement in the Conciergerie prison	Exiled to island of St. Helena
Death	1793, guillotine	1817, stomach cancer

ROBESPIERRE EXECUTED AS ENEMY OF THE REPUBLIC

At the height of the French Revolution in 1793, the eloquent Maximilien de Robespierre was the unofficial dictator of France. With the approval of the mob, he and his fellow members of the Committee of Public Safety instituted the infamous Reign of Terror in September 1793, whereby at least 17,000 supposed "enemies of the Republic" were executed and tens of thousands more were arrested and jailed in the span of just ten months. To assure expediency, those accused were denied a public trial and ultimately faced a Revolutionary Tribunal that decided between the death penalty and acquittal. Thus unencumbered, Robespierre's reign put hundreds of "enemies" to death each month, including many of his political rivals in the National Convention. But by mid-June 1794, Robespierre's health began to fail, and influential members of the Convention took advantage of his weakness. Politicians publicly spoke against him, and the radical citizens in the cafés accused him of being a "moderate." The political upheaval was complete on July 26, 1794, when Robespierre's speech in front of the National Convention met with disapproval from the parliamentary majority. The next day, the Convention declared Robespierre an enemy of the Republic. Desperate, he and his followers congregated in the Hotel de Ville, where Robespierre shot himself in the jaw in a failed suicide attempt. He was arrested, and after making a brief appearance in front of the Revolutionary Tribunal he'd helped create, he was guillotined in front of a cheering mob on July 28, 1794. **History Lesson:** Turnabout's fair play.

MAXIMILIEN DE ROBESPIERRE

President of the French National Convention; leader of Committee of Public Safety and General Police Bureau

BEST KNOWN FOR: Leading the "Reign of Terror" • Suspending suspects' right to a public trial • Creating Revolutionary Tribunal • Forcing French people to worship "Supreme Being" he invented

BORN: 1758, in Arras, France

FAMILY: Son of lawyer, who deserted his family of four upon wife's death. Raised by two aunts. Lived with his sister during his twenties; never married.

PHYSICAL DESCRIPTION: 5'3" tall, slight build, light brown hair, wore green-tinted glasses, meticulously dressed. Nervous tic caused his neck to turn, fists to clench, and eyes to blink rapidly.

EDUCATION: Early studies at Oratorians in Arras; law degree at Louis-le-Grand in Paris, where he once gave speech to welcome Louis XVI and Marie Antoinette

FIRST JOB: Lawyer

NICKNAME: The Incorruptible

LEAST KNOWN FOR: Original opposition to death penalty; fighting for universal suffrage, rights of Jews, and black slaves; his love of oranges

QUOTE: "Terror is nothing other than justice, prompt, severe, inflexible; it is therefore an emanation of virtue. . . ."

DEATH: 1794, beheaded by guillotine

SWEATIN' TO THE OLDIES

THE INDUSTRIAL REVOLUTION

1785   Edmund Cartwright's power loom puts hand-loom weavers out of business

1810   Miguel Hidalgo y Costilla launches revolution in Mexico

1811   Luddite movement begins in England

1812   U.S. declares war on Britain; invades their Canadian colony

1815   Napoleon defeated at Waterloo; exiled

1819   Beethoven loses hearing

1821   Spain loses Mexican colony in their war of independence

1830   France occupies Algeria

1833   English Factory Act requires children to be at least 9 years old to work

1836   Samuel Colt invents revolver

1842   China loses first Opium War to England

1845   Irish Potato Famine begins

1846   **April:** U.S. declares war on Mexico
         November: Donner Party of 87 pioneers are trapped in Sierra Mountains in winter, 41 die

1848   Revolutions erupt in Europe to limit power of monarchies
         January: Gold discovered in California
         February: Mexico cedes Texas, New Mexico, and California to the U.S.

1849   Cholera outbreak kills 13,000 Londoners

1853	English Factory Act limits work week to 72 hours
1854	Britain and France join the Ottoman Empire against Russia in the Crimean War
1858	Britain imposes formal colonial rule on India
1860	Gaslight allows British factories to work all night **November:** Abraham Lincoln elected president of U.S. **December:** Southern states secede from Union
1861	**April:** American Civil War begins **December:** Britain's Prince Albert dies; Queen Victoria wears black for her remaining 40 years
1862	**September:** French takeover of Indochina begins **November:** Dr. Richard Gatling patents the machine gun
1863	Battle of Gettysburg, bloodiest battle in American Civil War
1865	Abraham Lincoln assassinated
1868	Alfred Nobel receives U.S. patent for dynamite
1869	Transcontinental railway completed in U.S., thousands die in the making
1877	Southern Reconstruction ends in U.S. when Republicans make concessions to Southern Democrats
1878	French make first attempt at building Panama Canal; 20,000 die from disease
1884–1885	Imperial powers partition Africa without regard to the territorial claims of native inhabitants
1893	One-fifth of U.S. workforce unemployed after financial panic
1898	U.S.S. *Maine* sinks in Havana Harbor; Spanish-American War begins

YELLOW FEVER LEADS TO U.S. EXPANSION

In 1801, Napoleon Bonaparte had grand plans for extending the French empire not just in Europe but all over the world. In North America, he was starting with the reclamation of the island of Saint-Domingue (now Haiti) from black leader Toussaint-Louverture, who had declared himself the island's governor-general after taking charge of a slave rebellion. Napoleon sent his brother-in-law, General Charles LeClerc, with an army of 20,000 troops to recapture the island. LeClerc and his men arrived in Saint-Domingue in January 1802 and quickly gained the upper hand. But as LeClerc waited for the reinforcements that would finalize the French victory, the rainy season arrived, bringing with it a plague of mosquitoes and yellow fever. By June, 30 to 50 French soldiers were dying from the fever each day. LeClerc wrote to Napoleon with grave concern—though he'd captured Toussaint-Louverture, the sick French soldiers were unable to keep order. LeClerc himself died of the fever in October 1802, and his replacement, General Rochambeau, watched as 20,000 more soldiers were taken by the disease the following year, forcing France to give up the island in November 1803. Napoleon abandoned his North American plans in despair over the loss. He sold the United States the French-held Louisiana Territory at a bargain price of less than three cents an acre just to keep the land out of the control of Great Britain, France's biggest enemy. The new land doubled the size of the United States, gave the new country control over the Mississippi River and the important port of New Orleans, and allowed for continued westward expansion and exploitation of resources.

History Lesson: One man's misfortune is another man's opportunity.

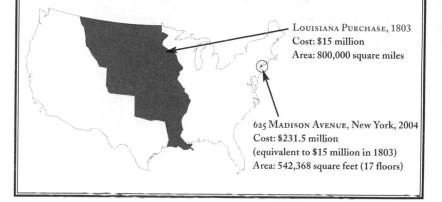

COST OF LOUISIANA PURCHASE VS. REAL ESTATE TODAY

LOUISIANA PURCHASE, 1803
Cost: $15 million
Area: 800,000 square miles

625 MADISON AVENUE, New York, 2004
Cost: $231.5 million
(equivalent to $15 million in 1803)
Area: 542,368 square feet (17 floors)

THE FIRST 30 DAYS

HARRISON GIVES INAUGURAL ADDRESS, DIES

Elected in 1840 on the strength of his record in the War of 1812, William Henry Harrison was determined to show the country how tough he was despite his 68 years. Even though the day of his inauguration was raw, cold, and wet, with heavy rains pelting down throughout the morning, he took off his coat and gloves and delivered a 105-minute speech, the longest inaugural address in American history. The next day he fell sick with a cold that progressed into pneumonia, despite his doctors' attempts to cure him with castor oil, calomel, ipecac, opium, camphor, and brandy. Within a month he became the first American president to die in office.

History Lesson: Be brief when giving speeches.

HOW TO CIRCLE THE WAGONS

1 | Choose the campsite.
At about 5 P.M. each day, choose a location to camp for the night. The area must be relatively flat, with good sight lines in all directions and ample grass and water for livestock. Avoid circling at the bottom of hills that would allow your enemies to gain elevation and attack the wagons from above.

2 | Slow the wagons.
Though most wagons will be pulled by oxen traveling two miles per hour at their fastest clip, gradually slowing to a halt will avoid any potential for collision.

3 | Halt the first wagon.
Direct the lead wagon to stop at an angle.

4 | Pull up the second wagon.
Drive the second wagon in the caravan next to the parked wagon, stopping it with its inside back wheel next to the outside front wheel of the first wagon.

5 | Complete the enclosure.
Continue parking the remaining wagons as described in steps 3 and 4 until a circle or oval is formed.

Align the back inside wheel of the first wagon with the outside front wheel of the next. Repeat to form the circle.

Send guards outside the circle after supper.

6 Unhitch the oxen, mules, and horses.
Before sealing the circle, move all the pack animals outside the circle. In instances when your caravan suspects a night attack, herd the animals inside the wagon perimeter rather than allowing them to graze outside.

7 Lock the wagon wheels together.
To fortify your temporary stockade, chain the wheels of the neighboring wagons together.

8 Post guards.
After supper, as the camp gets ready for bed, station guards just outside the circle to watch for danger. Every man in the camp will take a turn on guard duty. At midnight, a new set of guards should relieve those who went on duty after dinner.

BRITAIN FORCES CHINA TO LEGALIZE OPIUM

In the early 1800s, China was a self-sufficient nation, closed to foreigners, whose only official interest in dealing with Western countries was in exporting them tea and silk. But many Chinese citizens had an illicit opium habit, and England's colonization of India provided them with fields of opium-bearing poppies that helped even out the trade imbalance. By the mid 1830s, due to the ready supply of opium smuggled into the country on British merchant ships, China had as many as 12 million habitual opium users. To counter the negative social and economic effects of the widespread addiction, in 1839 the Chinese government imposed severe penalties for those caught selling or smoking opium. The British ignored the strengthened laws and continued to ply their trade until Lin Tse-hsu, Imperial Commissioner at Canton, seized and destroyed 20,000 chests of opium from British merchants and closed the country to trade of any kind. Fighting erupted, and by 1842 the technologically advanced British easily defeated the outmoded Chinese army. The Royal Navy sailed up the Yangtze River and forced China to accept the harsh terms of the Treaty of Nanking, which gave England sovereign control of Hong Kong among other terms highly favorable to the British. The opium trade remained an open issue, and more fighting broke out just 15 years later. This time France allied with the British, and the Chinese army suffered another defeat. In the Convention of Peking in 1860, China agreed to legalize the importation of opium. But the British plan backfired—after legalizing the drug, Chinese officials encouraged local cultivation of poppies, providing addicts with a cheaper, homegrown source and bolstering their economy. Within 20 years of the Convention of Peking, Britain's opium sales to China were seriously on the decline.

History Lesson: Be careful what you wish for.

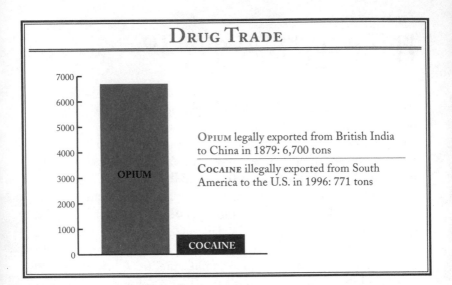

DRUG TRADE

OPIUM legally exported from British India to China in 1879: 6,700 tons

COCAINE illegally exported from South America to the U.S. in 1996: 771 tons

THE AGE OF THE SERIAL KILLER

Name	Method	Number of Victims
H. H. Holmes	Gas, strangling, live burial, stabbing	As many as 200
Mary Ann Cotton	Poisoning	18 (3 husbands, 15 of her own children)
Jack the Ripper	Strangling or throat-cutting, mutilation of corpse	5–13
Joseph Vacher	Stabbing, then disembowelment	11
Martin Dumollard	Stabbing or strangling, striking with blunt object	10
Eusebius Pieydagnelle	Stabbing, then drinking blood	6

HOW TO COVER UP THE DISCOVERY OF THE MOTHER LODE

✪ Say nothing.
Bragging about your mother lode is sure to get it noticed—and may get you into trouble with unsavory speculators who will try to "jump" your claim, steal your gold or other possessions, or even murder you.

✪ Hide your gold.
Stash the gold you've pulled from the river or ground beneath the floorboards of your cabin or underneath your tent, inside your pillow, in a hollowed-out tree stump, or in a hole outside the camp. If you hide it in an area accessible to others, make sure you choose a location unlikely to be claimed by another miner, and cover your tracks to avoid drawing attention.

✪ Make a show of poverty.
Borrow money and beg for drinks at the local saloon. Do not gamble or spend wildly.

✪ File another claim.
Divert attention from the mother lode by filing a second claim far from your successful mine. If your newfound wealth is revealed, announce that this second claim is where you've made your big discovery. This will attract miners to the more remote claim and away from your real findings. Continue to work both claims; if you

Hide your gold under your tent, in a hollowed-out tree stump, or outside the camp. Cover your tracks to avoid drawing attention.

spend too much time away from your original success-ful claim, it may legally be claimed by someone else due to your abandonment.

★ Sell something else.

You can often make more money supplying prospectors than by panning for gold. Corner the market in a criti-cal product (shovels, pans, lumber) and then charge obscene prices for these goods. Though you will be reviled as a price gouger, no one will suspect that you are sitting on the mother lode.

Gold Rush Place Names

Bean Pot
Chicken Thief Flat
Dirty Sock
Devil's Basin
Gouge Eye
Ground Hog Glory
Hell's Delight
Jackass Gulch
Lazy Man's Canyon
Lousy Ravine
Lucky Boy
Poverty Hill
Skinflint
Total Wreck
Whiskeytown

Bloody Canyon
Contention City
Frying Pan River
Git-up-and-Git
Greaser's Camp
Hangtown
Humbug
Last Chance
Loafers' Retreat
Love Letter Camp
One Horse Town
Rough and Ready
Spar City
Vulture City
Whorehouse Gulch

Nota Bene

Many famous companies, and the men who founded them, got their start supplying prospectors, including Levi Strauss (canvas pants), Henry Wells and William Fargo (banking and transportation), and John Studebaker (automobiles).

SUPREME COURT RULES IN FAVOR OF SLAVE OWNERS, CAUSES CIVIL WAR

When the lawyers completed their arguments for *Dred Scott v. Sanford* in December 1856, all of America waited for the Supreme Court's ruling. Dred Scott was a slave suing for his freedom, charging that the several years he'd spent in the free territories of Illinois and Wisconsin with army surgeon Dr. John Emerson gave him the legal right to make a bid for freedom. On March 7, 1857, the nine members of the court—seven of whom were appointed by proslavery, Southern presidents, and five of whom had come from slave-holding families—handed down a ruling that denied Scott's appeal for freedom. Chief Justice Taney's majority opinion declared that no black—not even free blacks—could be citizens of the United States, and therefore they had no right to bring lawsuits in federal court. He also stated that Congress had stepped beyond its constitutional limits in restricting the expansion of slavery in the Missouri Compromise of 1820, opening the door for slavery in territories where it had previously been forbidden. Such a bold reversal of Congressional authority increased the intensity of the debate over slavery around the country, ultimately helping Republican Abraham Lincoln win the 1860 presidential election, which in turn led to the South's secession from the Union. Dred Scott's personal battle ended on a brighter note—while Scott's case made its way through the courts, his owner, Mrs. Anderson, married a northern congressman opposed to slavery. She sold Scott and his wife and daughters to the family who had paid for his legal fees, who in turn gave the Scotts their freedom.

History Lesson: Sometimes one step forward requires two steps back.

BLOODIEST BATTLES OF THE AMERICAN CIVIL WAR

Name	State	Date	Casualties by Army	Total Casualties
Gettysburg	PA	July 1–3 1863	Union: 23,049; Confederate: 28,063	51,112
The Seven Days Battle	VA	June 25–July 1 1862	Union: 15,849; Confederate: 20,614	36,463
Vicksburg Campaign	MS	May 18–July 4 1863	Union: 4,550; Confederate: 31,275	35,825
Chickamauga Campaign	GA	Sept. 18–20 1863	Union: 16,170; Confederate: 18,454	34,624
Spotsylvania Court House	VA	May 8–21 1864	Union: 18,000; Confederate: 12,000	30,000
The Wilderness	VA	May 5–7 1864	Union: 18,400; Confederate: 11,400	29,800
Chancellorsville	VA	April 30–May 6 1863	Union: 16,792; Confederate: 12,764	29,556
Antietam (Sharpsburg)	MD	Sept. 16–18 1862	Union: 12,410; Confederate: 13,724	26,134
Second Manassas	VA	Aug. 29–30 1862	Union: 16,054; Confederate: 9,197	25,251
Shiloh (Pittsburg Landing)	TN	April 6–7 1862	Union: 13,047; Confederate: 10,694	23,741

HOW TO REPAIR SHOES WITHOUT LEATHER

1 Find soles.
At the end of a battle, scavenge the battlefield for a pair of shoes with the soles still intact. Place the soles against your feet to determine if they will fit you. If they are of an approximately correct size and the uppers appear also to remain intact, simply put them on and return to your company. If the uppers have separated from the soles, bind them to your feet with thick twine until you have time to continue with the repairs described in the following steps.

2 Remove the leather uppers.
Using your bowie knife, cut away torn, burned, or moldy leather from the soles and discard.

3 Make new uppers.
Using your knife, cut a piece of sturdy canvas (from an enemy tent or haversack) to approximately 14 inches square. Cut a hole approximately 4 inches in diameter a few inches from one edge; make sure the hole is large enough to accommodate your foot. Repeat with a second piece of canvas.

4 Position foot.
Place your right foot through the hole in one of the canvas pieces, then position the sole of your foot flat on the

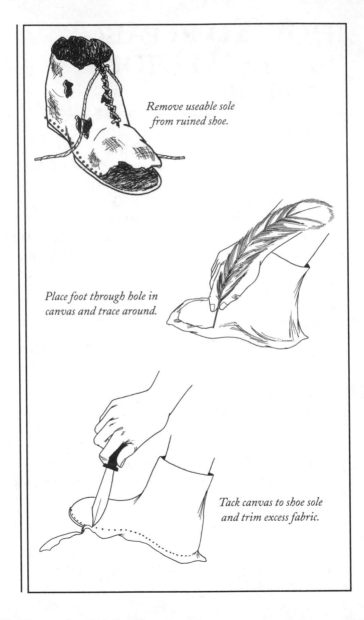

Remove useable sole from ruined shoe.

Place foot through hole in canvas and trace around.

Tack canvas to shoe sole and trim excess fabric.

sole of the shoe. Place the canvas "upper" over your foot and press it down so it is snug. Trace around your foot with a pencil or piece of charcoal. Remove your foot. Repeat for left foot.

5 | Tack.
Use small tacks or nails to secure the sheets of canvas to the soles. Position the tacks just outside the traced line on the canvas.

6 | Test fit.
Place your feet in the shoes and reposition and retack the canvas uppers if necessary for comfort. Cut away the excess canvas with your knife.

Nota Bene

Because of a severe leather shortage in the South, Confederate soldiers were often forced to go barefoot. These "barefoot brigades" were organized under separate commands and marched on the grass next to roads.

The battle of Gettysburg, one of the fiercest battles of the American Civil War, began because of the Confederate Army's desperate need for shoes. Confederate Major General Henry Heth discovered that there was a large supply of shoes stored in the town of Gettysburg; he marched 7,500 of his men toward the town to take them. They encountered enemy forces three miles from town, and the bloody three-day battle began.

WHO HAD IT WORSE?

	President Lincoln	President Garfield
Method of Assassination	1 shot with Derringer pistol	2 shots with British Bulldog pistol
Location of Wound	Bullet entered left ear, lodged behind eye	1st bullet grazed arm, 2nd bullet entered back
Time before Death	9 hours	80 days
Cause of Death	Hemorrhage	Infection from doctors' unsanitized fingers/instruments
Time in Office	4 years and 1 month	6 months
Age	56	49
Location at Time of Shooting	Ford's Theatre, Washington, DC	Train station, Washington, DC
Location at Time of Death	Peterson House, Washington, DC	Elberon, New Jersey
Name of Shooter	John Wilkes Booth	Charles Guiteau
Reason for Assassination	Booth and conspirators wanted to throw country into political chaos due to South's defeat in Civil War	Guiteau was insane, wanted appointment to be consul general of Paris

GENERAL GEORGE ARMSTRONG CUSTER

U.S. Army Cavalry Commander

BEST KNOWN FOR: Leading his 210 soldiers into a massacre by 4,000 Cheyenne and Sioux warriors at Little Bighorn • Burning 400 square miles of farms in Ohio in Civil War • Massacre of 153 Cheyenne in village at Washita River

BORN: 1839, in New Rumley, Ohio

FAMILY LIFE: Father was a blacksmith and farmer. Brothers Thomas and Boston died with him at Little Bighorn. Devoted to wife Elizabeth Bacon Custer.

PHYSICAL DESCRIPTION: Long, golden hair, drooping handlebar mustache. Wore black velveteen uniform trimmed in gold lace, wide-collared sailor shirt with silver stars, and red necktie.

EDUCATION: U.S. Military Academy at West Point; graduated last in his class, with 726 demerits, one of the worst disciplinary records in the Academy's history

FIRST JOB: School teacher in Ohio

NICKNAMES: Autie, Boy General, Old Curley

LEAST KNOWN FOR: Leading expedition that discovered gold in the Dakota territory in 1874, triggering the Black Hills Gold Rush

QUOTE: "There are not enough Indians in the world to defeat the Seventh Cavalry."

DEATH: June 25, 1876, at the Battle of Little Bighorn. Shot in the temple and the chest.

INDIAN TERRITORY NOW AND THEN

Land Held by Native Americans in 1500

Land Held by Native Americans in 1850

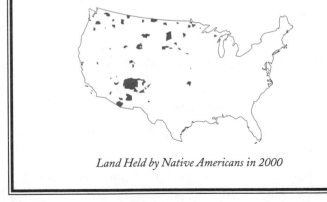

Land Held by Native Americans in 2000

ENGLISH HUNTER CAUSES ECOLOGICAL MELTDOWN

Thomas Austin, a wealthy rancher who'd settled in southeastern Australia, was an avid sportsman, and in 1859 he asked his brother James to send him 24 of the wild gray rabbits he'd grown up hunting and shooting in England. Austin released the rabbits on his estate on Christmas Day, 1859, and it didn't take long for the rabbit population to thrive. Since the rabbits had no natural predators on the continent, there was nothing to stop them from multiplying—and quickly, as female rabbits can have as many as six litters of three to four babies each year. Austin was proud of the success of the species he introduced, publishing tallies of the number of rabbits he hunted and killed each month—in the year 1867, he shot 14,362 on his own property! But the rabbits had spread beyond the borders of Austin's ranch and into the countryside, eating all the vegetation from farms and pastures along the way. Within 20 years, the rabbits had destroyed all the vegetation in a 500-mile radius—from January to August 1887, 10 million rabbits were killed in the state of New South Wales alone. In an attempt to block the rabbits' path into fertile Western Australia, a series of three rabbit-proof fences a total of 1,900 miles long were built by 1908, but the rabbits succeed in getting through anyway. By the 1940s, the country's rabbit population numbered in the hundreds of millions. Australians continue to fight rabbits to this day, using methods ranging from wire mesh, poison bait, traps, poison gas, and even viruses and biological agents. Rabbits cost Australia more than $456 million each year.

History Lesson: Think through your plan before acting.

HOW TO SURVIVE AS A CHILD LABORER IN A COAL MINE

★ **As a trapper:**
Trappers are responsible for opening and closing the canvas flap or door that regulates the ventilation of fresh air in the mineshafts. Sit in the hole in the wall on the side of the shaft and listen for the approach of a coal wagon. Pull the string and open the door to allow it to pass, closing it immediately after the coal wagon passes. Make sure you close the door tightly; if the ventilation is disrupted for a long period, you and the other miners may die from carbon monoxide poisoning or in a methane explosion. Ignore any rats that approach you in the tunnel—once they smell that you don't have any food to offer them, they will continue on their way.

★ **As a coal bearer:**
A coal bearer carries a coal-filled creel from the seam where the coal is mined up to the surface. A creel is a large basket fitted to the shape of the back that lies flat across the neck. The miners at the seam will fill your creel with 120 to 170 pounds of coal and then they will lift it onto your back, placing a strap over your forehead to help hold the creel in place. During the weight transfer, bend your legs and tighten your abdominal muscles to help provide support, then put your arms at your sides and use them to support the creel. Bend at the waist so that your torso is parallel to the floor to help

Trapper (left)

Coal Bearer

Thruster and Hurrier

maintain your balance on the wet ground. This also allows you to squeeze through the mineshafts, which are no more than 4 feet high. Remain in your hunched position and use your hands and leg muscles to climb the six to eight ladders or steep stairs connecting the tunnels to the surface. Keep your abdominal muscles tight during each of the journeys you make to prevent back injury.

⭐ **As a hurrier:**
Hurriers pull wagons full of coal to the mine's surface. Put on your leather harness and chain so that the chain passes through your legs and connects to the front of the coal-laden wagon. Pad the area where the harness presses against your shoulders and hips with extra cloth to stop the leather from digging into your skin and causing cuts or blisters. With the help of the thrusters behind you (see below), use the strength of your legs to pull the coal wagon up the 30-degree incline to the mine's surface. Crawl on your hands and knees to provide stability on the wet floor and to keep your back from aching since you will be unable to stand upright in the shaft.

⭐ **As a thruster:**
While the hurrier pulls from the front of the coal wagon, use your head, hands, and legs to push the load up the narrow paths to the surface of the mine. Turn your feet out at an angle to gain better traction as you push your way up the wet path. If the hurrier slips and you are unable to brace the load on your own, press yourself to the side of the tunnel and shout to warn the miners below of the careening coal cart.

★ | As a breaker boy:

You are responsible for bending down and picking out pieces of rock and slate from the coal that passes beneath your feet. Tie a piece of cloth around your nose and mouth to help filter some of the dust generated by the machinery. Do not lean too far over the line and risk losing your balance; it is better to let a piece of rock get by than to be smothered by the coal if you fall onto the chute. You will not be allowed to wear gloves, so beware the sharp edges of the coal and slate as you grab to try to minimize cuts and bleeding.

WORST JOBS OF THE 1800S

	Duties	Drawbacks
Chimney Sweep's Assistant	Climb into chimneys to clean soot	Chimney sweep sometimes lights match at feet to ensure your quick ascent; "chimney sweep's cancer," respiratory ailments, skin and eye inflammation from soot; broken bones from rooftop falls
Mill Scavenger	Brush cotton from beneath active textile machinery	Risk of being maimed by machinery without safety covering
Pure Collector	Gather dog and cat feces from streets for use by tanners in de-liming pools	Use of bare hands to collect feces
Stoker	Shovel coal into ships' steam engines	Extreme heat; risk of death from explosion underneath active textile machinery; risk of being maimed by machinery without safety covering
Tanner	Remove flesh and hair from cowhides, de-lime hides with animal excrement	Constant smell of aging excrement; contact with dead animals; tanneries located outside population centers
Thresher	Load bundles of wheat and barley into steam-driven threshing machine	Risk of being maimed by machinery without safety covering

HEROIN INTRODUCED AS NON-ADDICTIVE PAINKILLER, RESPIRATORY TREATMENT

In 1897, Germany's Bayer Pharmaceutical Products celebrated the synthesis of the world's newest miracle drug: Heroin. Though originally invented in 1874 by English chemist C. R. Wright, Bayer recognized Heroin's commercial potential not just as a painkiller but also as a cure for tuberculosis and pneumonia, the world's leading causes of death at the time. The drug was tested on Bayer's workers, and their response was overwhelmingly positive—they claimed the drug made them feel "heroic," and thus Heroin's trade name was born. Bayer approached members of the medical community, touting Heroin as a non-addictive substitute for morphine and codeine. The world's respected medical journals agreed, and Bayer soon sent free Heroin samples to doctors across Europe and the United States. The drug was especially popular in America, where Heroin was sold without a prescription in drugstores, groceries, general stores, and by mail order in any number of convenient forms—pills, lozenges, dissolvable tablets, and elixirs. But by 1902 doctors noted that some of their patients had developed a tolerance and a "hunger" for the supposedly non-addictive drug, and in 1906 the American Medical Association declared that Heroin was habit forming (though they still recommended use of the drug for its medical benefits). Hospitals in major U.S. cities were soon inundated with addicts. The United States banned the sale of Heroin without a prescription in 1914, and in 1924 it was outlawed altogether. But the profits of the Bayer company were unaffected by the prohibition on their invention. They had stopped producing Heroin in 1913, allowing other manufacturers to fulfill the world's appetite for the drug so they could concentrate on marketing their latest miracle invention—Aspirin.

History Lesson: If it seems too good to be true, it probably is.

CHINESE REBELS TAKE A STAND AGAINST FOREIGNERS

By the end of the nineteenth century, Japan, Russia, and the European colonial powers had forced numerous territorial and commercial concessions from the once fiercely independent nation of China. In reaction, anti-foreign sentiment spread throughout the country, leading to a rise in membership in I Ho Ch'uan (Righteous Harmonious Fists), a secret society nicknamed the "Boxers" by Westerners because of their use of ritualistic martial arts. The Boxers were opposed to foreign influence; in 1898 and 1899 they spread havoc across China, burning the homes and businesses of foreigners and killing missionaries and Chinese citizens who had converted to Christianity. Western officials protested the violence to the Chinese Dowager Empress, Tzu His, but she responded with tacit support of the Boxers' actions, hoping they could rid the country of foreign control. By May 30, 1900, the Boxers had arrived in Peking to terrorize Western dignitaries. Foreign ministers who resided in Peking's diplomatic quarter called on their militaries for help, but the Dowager Empress ordered the Imperial Army to force the international troops back to their ships. The diplomats and about 400 soldiers barricaded the streets of the diplomatic quarter to protect themselves, and the Boxers, allied with the Imperial Army, held them captive for 55 days. On August 15, 20,000 troops from Great Britain, Germany, Russia, France, the United States, Japan, Italy, and Austria marched into Peking to break the siege. The Dowager fled, aware that her plan had backfired; rather than freeing China of foreign influence, she'd provoked an invasion and opened the country to even stronger domination.

History Lesson: Fight the good fight, but be careful not to wake the sleeping giant.

Mottoes of the 1800s

Remember the Alamo!
Rally cry in Texans' battle with Mexican army in
their fight for independence

Remember the Maine, *and to Hell with Spain!*
Slogan run in newspapers to encourage U.S. participation in Cuban
fight for independence from Spain; refers to mysterious sinking of
USS *Maine* in Havana harbor before Spanish-American War

Sic Semper Tyrannis! (Thus Always to Tyrants)
John Wilkes Booth's utterance after shooting President Lincoln

Propaganda of the Deed
Anarchist rallying cry meaning that one violent action by an individual can lead others to take action as well

YOU SANK MY BATTLESHIP

THE EARLY 20TH CENTURY

1901	**January:** Queen Victoria dies **September:** U.S. president William McKinley assassinated
1905	First Russian revolution begins with "bloody Sunday"
1906	San Francisco earthquake destroys 28,000 buildings, leaving 225,000 homeless
1908	First airplane passenger killed
1912	RMS *Titanic*, "The Unsinkable Ship," sinks
1914	Austrian Archduke Franz Ferdinand assassinated; World War I begins
1915	**April:** Germans use chlorine gas against French troops on Eastern Front **May:** German U-20 sinks British ocean liner *Lusitania*
1916	Battle of Verdun; French lose 350,000 troops
1917	**October:** Mata Hari executed for spying **October:** V. I. Lenin instigates coup; declares Russia Communist state
1918	Influenza pandemic kills 20 to 40 million people **June:** U.S. Supreme Court invalidates first U.S. regulation of child labor, allowing children under 14 to go back to work **July:** Russian Czar Nicholas II and his family murdered
1919	Treaty of Versailles ends World War I, sets stage for World War II
1920	Prohibition begins in U.S.

1922	**June:** Irish Civil War begins
	October: King Emmanuel appoints Mussolini prime minister of Italy, gives him dictatorial powers
1923	Earthquake destroys Tokyo; kills more than 200,000, causes $1 billion in damage
1929	U.S. stock market crashes, beginning the slide into the Great Depression
1930	Nazis win 107 seats in German Parliament
1933	Nazis open Dachau, first concentration camp
1934	**May:** Worst drought in U.S. history creates "Dust Bowl" in Midwest
	December: Stalin begins major "purge"; 8 million killed, imprisoned, or sent to Siberia
1934	Hitler becomes president and chancellor of Germany
1936	Spanish Civil War begins
1937	**May:** Hindenburg zeppelin explodes
	November: Italy allies with Japan and Germany, establishing the Axis powers
1939	Germany invades Poland; World War II begins
1941	Japan draws U.S. into war by attacking fleet at Pearl Harbor
1945	**March:** Hitler issues "Nero Order" to destroy German infrastructure in advance of Allied invasion
	April: Hitler commits suicide
	May: Germany surrenders; war ends in Europe
	August: U.S. drops atomic bombs on Japanese cities of Hiroshima and Nagasaki and Japan surrenders

VOLCANO ERUPTS DESPITE POLITICIANS' ASSURANCES

During the first week of May 1902, as Martinique's Mount Pelée released a column of smoke, emitted sulfur fumes, produced ominous exploding sounds, and covered the French-Caribbean town of Saint-Pierre with ashes and cinders, the citizens were concerned— but not overly so. The older residents had seen the volcano erupt in 1851, but it had done no damage to the city, and they urged younger residents to remain calm. The local newspapers published columns ridiculing those who left in fear; a poster signed by the mayor assured citizens that the lava would never reach Saint-Pierre if an eruption occurred; and a scientific commission hired by the governor advised against evacuation, saying the city was completely safe. But on the morning of May 8, 1902, Mount Pelée exploded, blasting the city of Saint-Pierre for 3 whole minutes with a cloud of gas moving at 120 miles per hour, heated to temperatures of 700 to 1,300 degrees Fahrenheit. There was nothing the citizens of Saint-Pierre could do to escape—one breath of the superheated air seared their lungs and killed them. In the end, only two of the city's 28,000 inhabitants survived. One, a shoemaker, lived on the outskirts of town and was not exposed to the worst of the blast. The other, Auguste Ciparis, was right in the middle of it all—in solitary confinement. He'd been locked in a small jail cell with 12-inch-thick stone walls, a tiny window, and a small door. Though he was severely burned, he lived through the blast and was rescued three days later. After his recovery, he traveled the world with the Barnum & Bailey Circus as the "Sole Survivor of Saint-Pierre."

History Lesson: Trust your common sense.

HOW TO SURVIVE WHEN YOUR SHIP HITS AN ICEBERG

1 | Dress in your warmest clothes.
When the signal to abandon ship is given, or if you suspect that it will be given, put on multiple layers of clothes, preferably made of wool. Wear a hat and gloves, and wrap a scarf or a towel around your neck. Clothes offer the best protection against hypothermia if your rescue is delayed.

2 | Put on your life belt.
Cabins are equipped with life belts for each of the passengers; pull one over your head and securely fasten the straps. If you end up in the water, the life belt will provide additional buoyancy and allow you to save your energy for maintaining body temperature.

3 | Gather any portable, high-calorie foods.
Chocolates or candy are recommended. Put them in a pocket to give you energy later.

4 | Move to the top deck.
Quickly make your way to the uppermost deck of the ship, to put as much distance between yourself and the water as possible. If you are a first-class passenger, this will not be difficult, but if you are traveling third-class or in steerage, you may have to fight to reach the upper decks.

5 Get in a lifeboat.
Your best chance for survival is as a passenger on a lifeboat. Women and children will be taken onto the boats first.

6 If you cannot get into a lifeboat, jump into the water at the last possible moment.
A human can expect to live only 30 to 90 minutes in water 32° to 40°F. Remain on the ship until you see members of the crew jumping into the water; most crew members will be expected to stay with the ship until it's about to go under. Swim toward the lifeboats to increase your chance for rescue and to get far enough from the ship that you won't be pulled under when it goes down, but swim no farther than you have to, as any movement in cold water increases the rate of heat loss.

7 Make a makeshift life raft.
If you are unable to get onto one of the lifeboats, quickly locate a piece of floating debris to make into an emergency raft. An overturned boat, a door, or a large piece of wood are all good alternatives. If you can, find something that is large enough that you can completely climb out of the water and get on top of it, as cold water saps your body heat 25 times faster than air of the same temperature. If you can still feel your hands, wring out your wet clothes to increase their insulating value.

8 If you cannot locate debris, assume the heat escape lessening posture (HELP).
Cross your ankles, draw your knees to your chest, and cross your arms over your chest. Keep your hands high

Maintain body heat in the HELP position.

on your chest or neck to keep them warm. Remain as still as possible, as movement will drain body heat.

9   Once you are rescued, look for signs of hypothermia. Slurred speech and a lack of shivering are signs of severe body-temperature loss.

10   Immediately rewarm your body.
Remove your wet clothing and wrap your body in several layers of warm, dry clothing. Drink warm beverages, but avoid coffee, tea, or alcohol, as they will contribute to dehydration.

Be Aware

- Cardiac arrest can occur immediately upon exposure of the head and chest to cold water, due to a sudden increase in blood pressure. Respiratory shock can also occur, wherein the cold water causes the trachea to close, making it impossible to breathe.

- A sinking ocean liner creates a column of air bubbles above it, so people who get pulled under are falling through air rather than water, decreasing their chance to resurface and survive.

Nota Bene

A block of sea ice just a few yards in diameter can weigh several tons, enough to damage the hull of any ship not designed for icebreaking. While modern radar has made spotting large icebergs easier, during heavy seas small bergs may be hidden in the troughs between swells.

ARCHDUKE'S VACATION SPARKS WORLD WAR I

Though they were visiting under the auspices of official state business, the trip Archduke Franz Ferdinand and his wife, Sophie, took to Sarajevo in June 1914 was a welcome escape from the stifling judgments of Viennese society. Even though Sophie had been born into a noble Czech family, the snobbish Austrian elite never considered her an appropriate match for the heir to the Austro-Hungarian throne—in Vienna, she was not permitted to sit near her husband at state dinners, in his box at the opera, or in the car with him in royal processions. Sarajevo was far from the Viennese court, however, and on June 28 the couple enjoyed the rare treat of riding side by side. But in Sarajevo they faced a greater danger than being shunned by the ruling class—a group of radicals agitating for a unified Serbian state had lined the streets to assassinate Franz Ferdinand as a political protest. Early in the car's route one of the radicals threw a bomb at the archduke, but the vehicle escaped unharmed. Spooked but determined, the party continued with their day, altering their itinerary to include a visit to those injured in the morning's bombing. The change in plans disrupted the assassins' plot, and the royal couple probably would have escaped unharmed if their driver hadn't missed a turn. In an unlucky coincidence, he stopped on the street not five feet from conspirator Gavril Princip, giving him a perfect shot. Princip fired twice, hitting the archduke in the neck with one bullet and severing an artery in Sophie's groin with the other. Both were dead within several hours. Three weeks later, the Austro-Hungarian emperor blamed the assassination on the nation of Serbia, and within the week all of Europe was embroiled in the Great War. **History Lesson:** You can't run from bad luck or blame.

World Leaders Assassinated 1895–1914
(Without Starting a World War)

Name	Title	Country	Year
Sadi Carnot	President	France	1894
Stefan Stambolov	Prime Minister	Bulgaria	1895
Min	Queen	Korea	1895
Nasser-al-Din	Shah	Persia	1896
Antonio Cánovas del Castillo	Prime Minister	Spain	1897
Juan Idiarte Borda	President	Uruguay	1897
José María Reina Barrios	President	Guatemala	1898
Elizabeth ("Sissi")	Empress, Queen	Austria	1898
Ulises Heureaux	President	Dominican Republic	1899
Umberto I	King	Italy	1900
William McKinley	President	U.S.	1901
Aleksandar Obrenoviç	King	Serbia	1903
Charles	King	Portugal	1908
Luis Felipe	Crown Prince	Portugal	1908
Boutros Ghali Pasha	Prime Minister	Egypt	1910
Pyotr Arkadyevich Stolypin	Prime Minister	Russia	1911
José Canalejas	Prime Minister	Spain	1912
Francisco Madero	President	Mexico	1913
Manuel Enrique Araujo	President	El Salvador	1913
George I	King	Greece	1913

HOW TO SURVIVE IN A TRENCH

⭐ Resist the urge to peek over the parapet.
The parapet, or the side of the trench facing the enemy line, is protected by a wall of sandbags that offer some protection from stray bullets, but little from snipers and none from artillery shrapnel. Avoid raising your head or limbs over the parapet. Snipers are taking constant aim at your trench and will shoot if you expose yourself for even a fraction of a second.

⭐ Stay alert during "stand to."
An hour before dawn and dusk, sergeants on both sides will wake the troops to stand guard against a dawn attack, called "stand to." Be vigilant while standing on the fire step, have your rifle loaded and your bayonet fixed, and be ready to fight at a moment's notice.

⭐ Listen for the "plop" that precedes enemy mortar.
Immediately before a mortar round is fired, you will hear the distinctive plop of the shell being loaded into the gun. If you hear the plop, warn your comrades and immediately take cover in the dugout.

⭐ Protect yourself against poison gas.
Put on your gas mask when you hear the sentry blow his whistle. If you don't have your gas mask, dip a cotton pad in bicarbonate of soda and hold it over your face. If you are not assigned to man the line, take refuge in the

Put on your gas mask when the sentry blows his whistle.

dugout or seek shelter outside the low-lying trench, where gas will collect. Once the gas has dispersed, remnants of gas may still be on your boots. Wash them thoroughly before going behind the gas curtain in the dugout or you may trap the gas inside, harming you and your fellow soldiers.

★ If you meet an enemy patrol in No Man's Land, do not shoot.

Using your gun while in No Man's Land (the area between your trench and the trench of the enemy) will provoke machine gun fire from the trenches that will kill you as well as your enemy. Instead, wait to see if the other side wants to fight; you may allow one another to go about your business. If a fight ensues, engage in hand-to-hand combat or immediately run back to the trench with your entire party and start firing.

★ Prevent lice infestation.

Body lice lay their eggs in the seams of uniforms; kill them with exposure to intense heat, such as a lit candle, but do not hold the flame near the seam so long that the clothing catches on fire. Do this often, since it is impossible to kill all the lice and their eggs without disinfecting the clothes in boiling water, which is not available in the trench. Shave your head to prevent head lice.

★ Keep your feet dry.

Trench foot is caused by a fungus bred by the unsanitary conditions in the trenches. The infection enters the body through broken or blistered skin on wet feet and causes severe pain and disfigurement, which may lead to gangrene and amputation. To avoid getting trench foot, change your socks frequently, at least twice per day, but more often if dry socks are plentiful. Each morning and evening, coat feet with whale oil to help repel moisture.

★ Kill rats.
Trenches are infested with thousands of rats that eat dead bodies and spread disease. Stab them with your bayonet and throw the carcasses into No Man's Land. Do not shoot rats with your gun, as it is prohibited.

★ Complete your chores during the day.
Fighting is usually restricted to the nighttime, because the threat of snipers makes it too dangerous to operate in the light. Therefore, trench upkeep is ordered during the day; you may be assigned to refill sandbags with earth, repair the duckboards (wooden slats) that line the bottom of the trench, prepare the latrines, or drain the trench using pumping equipment. Pumping is especially important after a rainfall, because the walls will turn to mud and the water will collect in the bottom of the trench.

★ Sleep when you can.
After you complete your chores, steal a few minutes of sleep in the dugout to keep yourself rested and alert.

GERMAN EMPEROR HELPS TO CREATE SOVIET UNION

Vladimir Ilich Lenin, leader of the Bolsheviks, was stuck in Switzerland when Russia erupted in revolution in March 1917. Though he and his party had spent years discussing how to remove the czar from power, now that it was happening there was no way for him to travel across war-torn Europe without being arrested. Russia's allies, the French and British, had sworn to arrest all active revolutionaries, and the Germans and Austrians would never permit a Russian to move freely through their territories during wartime. However, Arthur Zimmerman, the undersecretary of state at the German Foreign Office, knew of Lenin's desire to return to Russia. He also knew that it was in Germany's interest to foment the Russian revolution—if Russia pulled out of the war due to domestic problems, Germany could consolidate its armies rather than waging war on two separate fronts. Zimmerman convinced the German Kaiser to give the Bolsheviks safe passage through Germany. On April 9, 1917, Lenin and 31 of his compatriots boarded a train in Berne and, with the Kaiser's blessing, set off for Petrograd by way of Germany and Sweden. To offset charges of treason and keep them legitimate in the eyes of the Russian people, Lenin and his group would not have to interact with any Germans on their journey—even their armed guards were only to speak to the Swiss Communist they'd brought to coordinate communication. They arrived in Petrograd on April 16, where Lenin was greeted by a cheering crowd. In October the Bolsheviks seized control of the government to create the Soviet Union, and by March 1918 Russia had withdrawn from the war, giving Germany control of the Ukraine, its Polish and Baltic territories, and Finland, and freeing the German soldiers from the Eastern front. **History Lesson:** Your enemy's enemy is your friend.

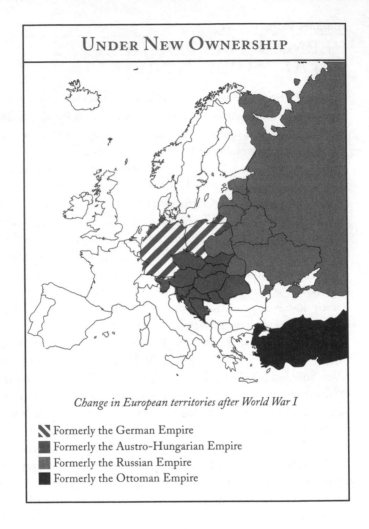

UNDER NEW OWNERSHIP

Change in European territories after World War I

- Formerly the German Empire
- Formerly the Austro-Hungarian Empire
- Formerly the Russian Empire
- Formerly the Ottoman Empire

ALPHONSUS CAPONE
Gangster, Chicago's Public Enemy Number 1

BEST KNOWN FOR: Leading Chicago's Prohibition-era mob • Masterminding the 1929 St. Valentine's Day Massacre, wherein seven rival gangsters were executed • Running speakeasies, gambling houses, nightclubs, race tracks, distilleries, and breweries

BORN: January 17, 1899, in Brooklyn, New York

FAMILY: Parents were Italian immigrants unassociated with criminal element; had eight siblings. Mary "Mae" Coughlin bore him a son, Sonny, on December 4, 1918; they were married on December 30.

PHYSICAL DESCRIPTION: Large, strong, round-faced; long scars from bar fight on left cheek

EDUCATION: B student until he was expelled from school at age 14

FIRST JOBS: Clerk in candy store, pinboy at bowling alley, worker at munitions factory, paper cutter at book bindery, bartender and bouncer at gangster Frankie Yale's Harvard Inn

NICKNAMES: Scarface, The Big Fellow

LEAST KNOWN FOR: Opening soup kitchens in Chicago after the 1929 stock market crash; ordering merchants to give clothes and food to the impoverished during the Great Depression at his expense

QUOTE: "I got nothing against the honest cop on the beat. You just have them transferred someplace where they can't do you any harm. But don't ever talk to me about the honor of police captains or judges. If they couldn't be bought, they wouldn't have the job."

DEATH: January 25, 1947, from cardiac arrest brought on by complications of a stroke and pneumonia

EARLY 20TH CENTURY FADS

Fad	When	What	Record
Dance Marathons	1920s and '30s	Couples danced as long as possible	5,148 hours
Flagpole Sitting	1920s	Sit atop a flagpole for as long as possible	49 days
Six-Day Bicycle Races	1920s and '30s	Teams of bikers raced on an indoor track for six straight days	N/A
Bunion Derbies	late 1920s	Foot race across U.S.	526 hours, 57 minutes, 30 seconds
Goldfish Swallowing	1939	Swallowing live goldfish	300 goldfish

HOW TO SURVIVE A DANCE MARATHON

⭐ Dress for endurance.
Wear comfortable shoes, loose trousers (for men), and a loose skirt or dress (for women). Bring several changes of clothes if you plan on participating in the marathon for more than 24 hours. Women should avoid wearing shoes with high heels.

⭐ Replenish fluids.
Dehydration is the biggest enemy of the dance marathoner. Drink one glass of water mixed with half a crushed banana and 1/2 teaspoon of salt per hour. Avoid coffee, which may make you feel more awake temporarily but will dehydrate you—and force you to use the bathroom more often.

⭐ Eat.
The marathon promoters will serve 12 meals each day, consisting of staples such as oatmeal, eggs, toast, oranges, and milk. The food will be placed on chest-high tables so you are able to continue moving while you eat. Make sure you eat your fill during each meal to replenish the nutrients you expend with your constant movement.

⭐ Stay loose.
Once every 24 hours, use one of your break periods to hire the masseuse provided by the marathon's promoter to ward off cramping and muscle fatigue.

Take mini naps.
You will be allotted 15 minutes off the dance floor per hour. Go to a quiet dressing room and nap during this period. Assign someone trustworthy to wake you up after 11 minutes to give you time to have a drink and use the bathroom. With this method, you will actually sleep almost 5 hours (total) out of every 24.

 Shuffle.
The rules demand only that you remain moving and keep your knees off the floor. When overcome by exhaustion, clutch one another and sway to and fro in a slow rhythm.

 Keep your partner awake.
Shake or pinch your partner if he seems to be drifting off, or if he starts to hallucinate or act hysterically. Pinpricks and slaps to the face can also help to bring him back to his senses.

 Take turns doing other things.
Late at night and during the day, when the paying crowds are thin or nonexistent, the rules allow you to pass the time doing any number of activities on the dance floor. Shave, read the newspaper, knit, or even write letters on a special folding desk hung around your own neck.

 Sleep while dancing.
During off hours, tie together the wrists of the person who is going to nap (the "lugger"), and slip his arms

Do not allow your sleeping partner's knees to touch the floor.

over the head of the partner who will remain dancing (the "carrier"). The partner responsible for staying awake should hold the other up to make sure his knees do not touch the floor.

Be Aware

- To make dance marathons more accepted by conservative churchgoers, they are often referred to as "walkathons" by the promoters who host them.
- A dance marathon can last for months.

Nota Bene

In the 1930s, dance marathons were huge moneymakers for their promoters, as Depression-era audiences paid to be entertained by the participants willing to push themselves to the limit for the opportunity to win a few hundred dollars. Some contestants participated in the marathons just for the opportunity to eat the meals provided by the promoters. By the postwar period, many states passed laws limiting the duration of marathons after several participants died from pushing themselves too far.

STOCK MARKET CRASH OF 1929

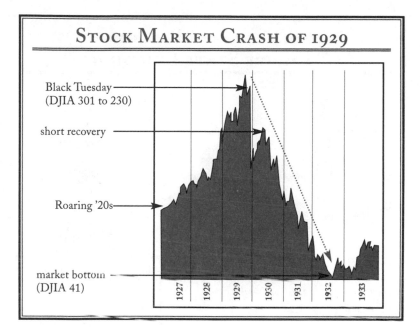

Black Tuesday
(DJIA 301 to 230)

short recovery

Roaring '20s

market bottom
(DJIA 41)

1927 1928 1929 1930 1931 1932 1933

WHAT A DIME WOULD BUY IN 1932

- 3 pounds apples
- 1 pound frankfurters
- 1/2 pound slab bacon
- 1/4 pound sliced bacon
- 1 pound ham
- 1 pound hamburger
- 1/2 pound bananas
- 6 lemons
- 2 loaves unsliced bread
- 1 loaf sliced bread

- 3 pounds cabbage
- 1 pound pork chops
- 3 candy bars
- 10 pounds potatoes
- 1/2 pound cheese
- 2 cans red beans
- Two 20-ounce packages flour
- 1/2 pound coffee
- 3.5 pounds oats
- 9 oranges

GOLDEN GATE BRIDGE VS. EMPIRE STATE BUILDING

	Golden Gate Bridge	Empire State Building
Location	San Francisco	New York City
Date Opened	May 27, 1937	May 1, 1931
Time to Build	3 years, 4 months, 3 days	1 year, 1 month, 15 days
Workers Killed During Construction	11	14
Cost	$79.5 million	$41 million
Height/ Length	1.7 miles long	1,250 feet high

UNITED STATES REFUSES TO EXPORT HELIUM, *HINDENBURG* BURNS

After the First World War, Dr. Hugo Eckener successfully mined the commercial potential of the hydrogen-filled flying machines the Germans had used to bomb England. However, Eckener recognized the danger of inflating dirigibles with highly flammable hydrogen gas and designed the *Hindenburg,* the world's largest airship, to use noncombustible helium instead. But the U.S. government had a monopoly on helium, and because of its potential use for combat, Congress had to approve any substantial export. When the United States denied Eckener the gas due to his company's affiliations with the Nazis, he inflated the *Hindenburg* with hydrogen instead, and by 1937 it had made 34 successful Atlantic crossings. But on May 6, 1937, as the zeppelin prepared to land in Lakehurst, New Jersey, the ground crew noticed a flutter in the ship's cover. A moment later, the entire ship was engulfed in fire, and within 32 seconds its skeleton lay smoldering on the ground. Twenty-six passengers were killed. Public outrage over the crash led many to pressure U.S. Secretary of the Interior Harold Ickes into selling Germany the helium, but before the pickup was made, Hitler annexed Austria, and Ickes rescinded the deal.

History Lesson: Never take short cuts when safety is at stake.

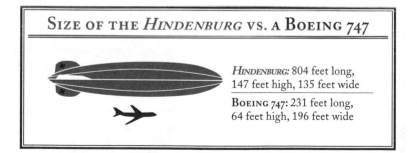

SIZE OF THE *HINDENBURG* VS. A BOEING 747

HINDENBURG: 804 feet long, 147 feet high, 135 feet wide

BOEING 747: 231 feet long, 64 feet high, 196 feet wide

ADOLF HITLER

Führer and Reich Chancellor

BEST KNOWN FOR: Murdering 11 million people, including 6 million Jews • Causing World War II, during which more than 50 million were killed • Overseeing creation of concentration and extermination camps

BORN: April 20, 1889, in Braunau am Inn, Austria

FAMILY: Father, Alois, a customs officer, was 23 years older than his third wife and second cousin Klara, Hitler's mother; met Eva Braun in 1930 but didn't marry her until the day before he committed suicide

PHYSICAL DESCRIPTION: Medium build, slender, tiny mustache, black hair, piercing dark eyes

EDUCATION: Didn't graduate high school; sought admission to the Vienna Academy of Fine Arts but was twice rejected

FIRST JOBS: Painting and selling postcards in Vienna; fighting in the German infantry in World War I

NICKNAMES: Wolff, Der Fuehrer

LEAST KNOWN FOR: His vegetarianism • Bathing several times a day • Regularly sleeping until noon • Bohemianism in his youth

FAVORITE PETS: Fuchsl, a small white terrier who joined him in the trenches in World War I; Blondi, German Shepherd who was his companion during World War II

QUOTE: "It is untrue that I, or anyone else in Germany, wanted the war in 1939. It was desired and instigated solely by those international statesmen who were either of Jewish descent or worked for Jewish interests."

DEATH: On April 30, 1945, with Russian troops just blocks from his bunker in Berlin, simultaneously shot himself in the head and bit an ampoule of cyanide. Eva Braun also committed suicide.

GERMANS INVADE FRANCE DESPITE FORTIFICATION

France suffered horrible losses, both in human lives and physical destruction, due to Germany's invasion in World War I. To ward off the potential for another German invasion, in the 1930s the French built a series of forts, outposts, and tank traps along their eastern border, stretching 150 miles from Switzerland in the south to Longuyon, near Belgium and Luxembourg, in the north. Named the "Maginot Line" after Defense Minister Andre Maginot, this engineering marvel consisted of more than 500 buildings, with some extending as far as six stories underground. A large fort was erected every 9 miles, with smaller outposts in between, all connected by a series of tunnels and underground trains. Everything necessary to sustain French soldiers was built underground—hospitals, supply warehouses, living quarters, recreation areas, and even air-conditioned galleries. But in May 1940, the German army invaded France despite the elaborate fortification. The Maginot Line only extended north to the Ardennes Forest, a hilly area thick with trees that the French military planners thought would provide a natural protection from the Germans. France and its allies knew the Germans were coming, but they all assumed the Germans would march through the flatlands of Belgium and hence the strongest troops were positioned to defend that area. Instead, the Germans did what the French thought impossible and came through the hole in the Ardennes, outflanking the line and meeting weak, inexperienced troops who were easy to overpower. When France surrendered to the Germans on June 22, 1940, the formidable Maginot Line remained fully intact.

History Lesson: Don't put all your eggs in one basket.

HOW TO SURVIVE AN AIR RAID

1 Stop what you are doing.
Authorities will sound the air-raid siren when enemy bombers are spotted in the skies. The warning siren changes pitch (from low to high) at a fixed interval, similar to the siren on a fire engine.

2 Put on your gas mask.
Don your government-issued gas mask to protect against a gas attack.

3 Move to an air-raid shelter immediately.
Gather children and anyone else in the household and get to the closest air raid shelter: a subway station, a reinforced railway arch (below ground), the basement of a large building, the cellar of your home, a public shelter, a backyard Anderson shelter (metal shelter dug halfway underground and covered with soil), an indoor Morrison shelter (table with a steel frame and welded mesh sides), or, as a last resort, underneath stairs in the house.

4 Wait.
Do not leave the shelter until you hear the "all clear" siren, a sustained monotone wail lasting several minutes.

5 Check your home for incendiary bombs.
Incendiary bombs are typically lightweight magnesium tubes that start fires rather than causing explosions.

Pump water onto an incendiary bomb to make it burn out faster.

Because they only weigh 2 to 5 pounds, they may only penetrate your roof as far as your attic or top floor. To deal with an incendiary bomb, put a stirrup pump into a bucket of water, stand on the metal leg to keep it still, then pump the handle to fill the hose with water. Direct the stream of water onto the bomb until the fire burns itself out. Putting water on magnesium will actually cause it to burn faster and therefore do less damage; without the water, the bomb could burn for 15 minutes, but with it, it will extinguish itself in a minute or two.

Now We Know

Few underground shelters, including those in subways, could withstand a direct hit or multiple hits from bombs. Occupants were sometimes killed in intact shelters when the buildings and machinery above them collapsed and fell, or blocked exits.

How to Prepare for an Air Raid

Carry your gas mask at all times.
Sling it over your shoulder and take it with you wherever you go. You never know when a gas attack may occur.

Pile sandbags around the house.
Fill bags with sand and put them around the exposed areas of the ground floor, barricading first-floor windows about halfway up.

★ Reinforce windows with tape.
The force of an exploding bomb can easily shatter windows. Criss-cross all window panes with 1 1/2-inch-wide tape to prevent glass from flying into the room.

★ Hang blackout curtains.
To keep enemy planes from seeing light through your windows and targeting your home, hang thick black curtains over every window. Use black tape to seal the edges where the curtain meets the wall to prevent even a crack of light from getting through. Air-raid wardens patrol the streets to make sure no light shows through; if you are caught ignoring their instructions, you can be fined.

★ Create a refuge room.
To protect yourself against a gas attack, fortify your cellar or the ground-floor room that has the fewest windows. Stuff paper into the chimney, seal cracks in the walls or ceiling with putty, tape around the edge of window frames, and plug keyholes in doors to keep air from coming through. Keep a bowl of water and a blanket at least 12 inches longer than the door in the room; in the event of an attack, wet the blanket and hang it over the door. Store old newspapers to stuff under the door after you're safely inside. Stock up on canned food and water, and keep a can opener and a radio in the room.

★ Take note of the closest air-raid shelters.
As you move about outside your home, look for signs directing you to the nearest shelter, whether it be a subway station, a shelter in a large department store, or a trench in the park.

Be Aware

At night streetlights are dimmed or turned off, and traffic lights are covered with hoods and painted black but for a small cross in their center. Cars must be fitted with slots for their headlights that deflect light downward, making it difficult to see. Driving at night is dangerous and best avoided if possible.

Nota Bene

On September 7, 1940, about 900 German planes stormed London in a massive daylight air raid, the first of 57 consecutive days of bombing. The bombing set London's piers alight and caused major damage to several areas of the city. More than 400 people were killed, and 1,300 injured. After this daring initial attack, most air raids occurred at night under cover of darkness. By the end of the summer of 1941, the Germans reduced the number of air raids on the British Isles to concentrate on Greece and the Eastern Front. During this period, called "the Blitz," more than 41,000 Londoners were killed, 49,000 were injured, and 46,000 dwellings were destroyed.

SCIENTISTS START UNSTOPPABLE NUCLEAR REACTION

In July 1939, Hungarian-born nuclear physicist Leo Szilard visited Albert Einstein with a desperate plea for help. Szilard was deeply concerned that the Nazis were developing a bomb that harnessed the energy created in a nuclear chain reaction, but the United States had no official program to do the same. Szilard had sought a meeting with Franklin Roosevelt to discuss the potential devastation such a bomb could create, but he was turned away. Einstein, as an internationally respected scientific genius, could wield influence that Szilard could not. Szilard showed Einstein a letter he'd written on his behalf urging the president to provide government funding for experiments in nuclear reaction. Though Einstein was a pacifist, he also feared Hitler's domination of such a destructive weapon, so he agreed to sign a revised version of Szilard's letter. Einstein's involvement convinced the president to create the Uranium Committee, which ultimately led to the creation of the Manhattan Project and the first atomic bombs. As the experiments proved successful, Szilard began to fear what he'd helped to create, and in early 1945 he asked Einstein to sign another letter urging President Roosevelt to listen to scientists' warnings. This letter went unanswered, however, as Roosevelt died before it was ever opened. When Germany surrendered in May, it became clear that German scientists had made little progress in developing atomic energy, making the United States the sole possessors of the technology. Nonetheless, President Harry Truman authorized the release of two atomic bombs in Japan in August 1945, killing tens of thousands of people and starting the nuclear arms race. For the rest of their lives, both Einstein and Szilard advocated for the peaceful international control of nuclear weaponry.

History Lesson: You can't put the toothpaste back in the tube.

JOSEPH STALIN

Secretary-General of the Communist Party of the
Soviet Union and Premier of the Soviet State

BEST KNOWN FOR: Killing more than 40 million of his own people •
Creating deliberate famine in the Ukraine • Deporting and imprisoning
better-off peasants in Gulag system • "Purging" intellectuals, party
bosses, military leaders, government officials, and general population •
Creating Iron Curtain at end of World War II

BORN: December 21, 1879, in Gori, Georgia

FAMILY: Domineering mother; beaten by father, a cobbler and an
alcoholic. Grew up poor. Married twice; second wife committed suicide
and left note blaming him. Three children; first son taken hostage by
Germans in World War II and Stalin refused offer for exchange.
Daughter defected to the West after his death.

PHYSICAL DESCRIPTION: Stocky, short, dark brown hair. Large
mustache to cover face scarred from bout of smallpox in infancy; left
arm a couple inches shorter than right.

EDUCATION: Mother wanted him to be a priest; attended parochial
school, then seminary on full scholarship but was expelled

FIRST JOBS: Errand boy at shoe factory where his father worked; tutor;
clerk in the Tiflis Observatory

LEAST KNOWN FOR: Singing in the seminary choir

NICKNAMES: Soso, Koba, Father Stalin, Uncle Joe

QUOTE: "Death solves all problems: no man, no problem."

DEATH: He died of a cerebral hemorrhage on March 5, 1953. His
body was entombed next to Lenin's in the mausoleum on Red Square in
Moscow.

SOVIETS WIN BIG AT YALTA

By February 1945, the Allies had gained the upper hand in the European theater of the Second World War—Italy had surrendered, and Germany was on its last legs. Winston Churchill, Franklin Roosevelt, and Joseph Stalin met at Yalta on the Crimean Peninsula to negotiate a plan for the occupation and reconstruction of Nazi-held territory upon the impending German surrender. But even though the war in Europe was soon to end, the American war in the Pacific was still raging, and Roosevelt feared the loss of several hundred thousand American lives in battles still to come. Despite Churchill's distrust of Stalin, Roosevelt was willing to take Stalin at his word if it meant maintaining their alliance and another army in the Pacific. In their negotiations, Stalin demanded that the Soviet occupation zone be extended to the Elbe River in eastern Germany; Roosevelt backed this under the condition that free representative elections be held in countries formerly under German control. Roosevelt also agreed that the USSR would recover the Asian territory lost to Japan in the Russo-Japanese War of 1904–1905. In exchange, the Russians would enter the war in the Pacific within 90 days of Germany's surrender. But in the end, all the Soviet appeasement proved to be unnecessary and even against American interests. The atomic bomb, America's new superweapon, rendered the Soviet alliance unnecessary—the Japanese surrendered before any Soviet soldiers ever fired a shot in the Pacific. And the "free" elections Stalin agreed to arrange in Poland, Czechoslovakia, Hungary, Romania, and Bulgaria were all fixed for Communist leaders, creating the Soviet bloc of the Cold War and extending the reach of Communist power.

History Lesson: Alliances are unpredictable.

CAN'T WE ALL JUST GET ALONG?

THE CONTEMPORARY WORLD

1946   Nine Nazi leaders hanged after Nuremberg trial

1947   Partition of newly independent India displaces 10 million

1948   **January:** Mahatma Gandhi assassinated
        May: Israel formed; war begins next day
        May: South Africa implements Apartheid policy

1949   Soviets successfully detonate atomic bomb

1950   North Korea invades the South, starts Korean War

1951   U.S. detonates first hydrogen bomb

1952   Joseph McCarthy obtains chairmanship of Government Committee on Operations of the U.S. Senate

1953   Julius and Ethel Rosenberg executed for selling A-bomb formula to Soviets

1961   Berlin Wall built

1962   U.S. discovery of Soviet missiles in Cuba take countries to brink of war

1963   U.S. president John F. Kennedy assassinated in Dallas, Texas

1964   U.S. Surgeon General issues first report on dangers of cigarette smoking

1965   Watts race riots in Los Angeles

1966   Mao Zedong's Chinese Cultural Revolution begins

SOVIET CLERK STARTS COLD WAR

On September 5 and 6, 1945, Igor Gouzenko, a 24-year-old cipher clerk at the Soviet Embassy in Ottawa, Canada, was bounced from the *Ottawa Journal* to the Canadian Ministry of Justice to the Crown Attorney's office as he offered to reveal hundreds of Soviet secrets in exchange for political asylum. He carried a bag with more than a hundred telegrams, reports, letters, and agent dossiers that he'd stolen from the embassy when he learned that he was being sent back to the USSR. Canada's prime minister, William Lyon Mackenzie King, had been told about Gouzenko but didn't want to get involved. Though the West was suspicious of the USSR, Stalin was still remembered as a wartime ally, and King did not want to offend him. But after a group of men from the Soviet Embassy ransacked Gouzenko's apartment, King's undersecretary for external affairs recognized that Gouzenko was in danger and authorized his defection. Gouzenko revealed that the Soviets were conducting a major espionage operation in the United States, England, and Canada, especially regarding military operations, and that they had obtained key secrets to the formula for the atomic bomb. In February 1946, Prime Minister King appointed a special commission to investigate the allegations, which ultimately led to the arrests of several scientists and government officials in Canada, England, and the United States. Gouzenko's testimony and paperwork established the Soviet Union as an enemy rather than a friend to the West, effectively starting the Cold War. Gouzenko and his family remained in Canada, using an assumed name for the rest of their lives.

History Lesson: You don't always know who your friends are.

HOW TO DEFECT FROM THE USSR

⭐ Give the impression of being a loyal and committed Communist.
Avoid drawing attention to yourself while planning your defection by appearing beyond reproach.

⭐ Develop your talents.
Ballet dancers, ice skaters, hockey players, circus performers, Olympic athletes, and members of the symphony and choir all tour outside of the USSR, an opportunity that presents the best chance for escape. Slip away from your handlers during a sightseeing trip and go to the nearest police station. Declare your intention to defect.

⭐ Join the foreign service.
Approach a Western diplomat and tell him of your intention to defect. Make sure no one can overhear you. Many embassy employees are actually agents with the CIA, and your message will quickly get to the proper levels. Follow instructions from your assigned handler, but resist Agency demands to remain in your current position and be run as a double agent.

⭐ Join the Soviet Air Force.
Fly a jet to a friendly country (Japan, Switzerland) and request political asylum. You will be most likely to succeed if you are flying a plane that is interesting to Western officials, such as a MiG-29, MiG-31, or Su-27.

When defecting, try to blend in.

★ Bribe officials.

Offer money to government officials or guards at checkpoints in return for forged traveling papers or identity cards. Make sure you know that the officials are likely to cooperate before offering the bribe; you may be shipped to Siberia or put in prison if you talk to the wrong person.

★ Go under the Wall.

Using contacts in East Germany, locate a building attached to a tunnel under the Berlin Wall. Such tunnels are discovered and filled regularly, so opt for newer passages that have recently been completed.

Be Aware

Defecting is least risky for unmarried, childless persons, as family members remaining in the Soviet Union may be sent to a gulag.

Famous Soviet Defectors

Name	Source of Fame	Year
Svetlana Alliluyeva	Writer, Joseph Stalin's daughter	1967
Mikhail Baryshnikov	Ballet dancer	1974
Viktor I. Belenko	Pilot	1976
Anatoly Kuznetsov	Writer	1969
Alexander Mogilny	Hockey player	1989
Rudolf Nureyev	Ballet dancer	1961
Oleg Protopopov and Ludmila Belousova	Ice-skating champions	1979
Arkady Shevchenko	Soviet Ambassador to the UN	1978
Maxim Shostakovich	Conductor, son of composer Dmitri Shostakovich	1981

Defected to	How
U.S.	Took a cab to the U.S. Embassy in New Delhi, India, when Soviet officials denied her request to extend her stay; went back to USSR in 1984
U.S.	Ran to a waiting car after Bolshoi Ballet's final performance in Toronto
U.S.	Made deal with CIA to fly MiG-25 plane to Japan in exchange for political asylum
UK	Asked handler if he could visit a prostitute; went to British government office instead
U.S.	Slipped away from 1989 World Championship Hockey Tournament, flew to New York's JFK airport
Austria	Jumped security barrier at Paris's Le Bourget airport saying "I want to be free!"; granted temporary asylum in France
Switzerland	Disappeared at end of tour of West Germany and Switzerland, resurfaced with amnesty
U.S.	Spied for U.S. for 3 years; slipped out of apartment at night to meet U.S. agents
U.S.	With his son, Dmitri, eluded guards at post-concert dinner party in Nuremberg, Germany; went to police station

B-52 WITH NUCLEAR WARHEADS CRASHES NEAR GREENLAND

On January 21, 1968, a B-52 from Plattsburgh Air Force Base, New York, crashed and burned on the Arctic Sea ice a few miles from the runway at Thule Air Base, Greenland. It was carrying four nuclear warheads, all of which were destroyed by fire. The nuclear material in the bombs did not explode, but the explosives in the outer coverings did, contaminating approximately 8,000 square miles with plutonium, uranium, tritium, and americium. Had a nuclear reaction taken place, the resultant explosion would have caused massive destruction of the area, cutting off communications between the nearby radar station and NORAD (North American Aerospace Defense Command). This would have triggered an emergency alarm prompting a quick and devastating nuclear response from the United States, who would have assumed the USSR had attacked with nuclear weapons.

History Lesson: Things could be worse.

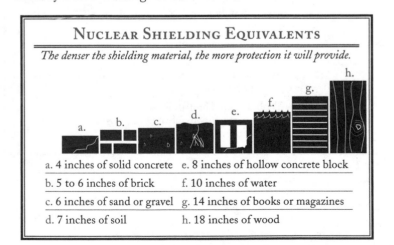

NUCLEAR SHIELDING EQUIVALENTS

The denser the shielding material, the more protection it will provide.

a. 4 inches of solid concrete	e. 8 inches of hollow concrete block
b. 5 to 6 inches of brick	f. 10 inches of water
c. 6 inches of sand or gravel	g. 14 inches of books or magazines
d. 7 inches of soil	h. 18 inches of wood

HOW TO CONSTRUCT AN EMERGENCY BASEMENT FALLOUT SHELTER

1 | Move a large, sturdy table or workbench into a windowless corner of the basement.
The table or bench must have enough room under it to shelter you and your family. If you are sheltering more than a couple of family members, or if you do not have a strong table or workbench, take a thick, solid door or doors off their hinges and place on top of dressers, bookcases, chests, trunks, etc.

2 | Pile shielding material on and around the table.
The denser the shielding material, the more protection it will provide. Use books, magazines, boxes filled with soil or sand, stacks of firewood or lumber, appliances, concrete blocks, bricks, full water containers, and boxes and pillowcases full of anything that has mass and can help absorb and deflect gamma particles. Cluster dressers and chests around the table and fill their drawers with sand or soil. Reinforce the center of the table with a piece of wood or another support to ensure that it doesn't collapse under the weight of the shielding materials. Leave at least two gaps for air spaces, more if there will be many of you in the shelter.

3 | Stock up on water.
Gather enough water and liquids to allow each person one quart of liquid each day for two weeks. Store the liquid in containers with tightfitting lids. Make sure you have at least three days' worth of water inside the shelter; the rest should be nearby. The water will be safe as long as it does not come into contact with the outside of the container, which may be covered with radioactive particles.

4 | Gather food.
Canned foods or foods in sealed packages that do not require refrigeration are preferable. Take a can opener into the shelter as well.

5 | Put a radio in the shelter.
In case of disaster, listen to the radio to find out when it is safe to move around. Also take extra batteries into the shelter.

6 | Cover basement windows.
If time allows, nail pieces of wood across windows to prevent breakage, then pile sandbags or shovel earth outside any basement windows and entrances.

7 | Seal yourself in.
Climb under the table, pull shielding material around the open space you crawled through, and listen to the radio for further instruction.

Insulate your shelter with as much shielding as possible.

Be Aware

- Air does not become radioactive; particles carried by the air, called fallout, are the cause of radiation problems. Due to variation in the direction of the wind at different altitudes, fallout can be deposited in irregular patterns hundreds of miles from the blast site.

- Nuclear fallout becomes less dangerous every hour after the initial explosion. Within two weeks, the radiation level will have decreased to $1/1000$ of the original rate of radiation, meaning that 99.9 percent of its strength will be gone. But the remaining 0.1 percent could be quite dangerous if the radiation was high at the start.

- If you do not have a basement, go to the closest structure with the greatest mass and distance between the outside where the fallout will settle and the inside where you will be sheltered. A multi-floor building may offer the best protection in the center of the middle floors, since it is distant from both the fallout on the ground and the fallout on the roof.

DESTRUCTION FROM NUCLEAR BLAST

| Nuclear Blast | → | 3 miles | → | 3 to 5 miles | → | 5 to 10 miles | → | 10 to 15 miles |

3 MILES: Complete destruction

3 TO 5 MILES: Damage beyond repair

5 TO 10 MILES: Major repairs required

10 TO 15 MILES: Light to moderate damage

WEAPONS IN NUCLEAR ARSENAL, 1986

Britain	▮	300
France	▮	355
China	▮	425
U.S.	▮▮▮▮▮▮▮▮▮▮▮▮▮▮▮	24,401
Russia	▮▮▮▮▮▮▮▮▮▮▮▮▮▮▮▮▮▮▮▮▮▮▮▮▮▮▮▮▮▮▮	45,000

OSS SAVES LIFE OF FUTURE ENEMY

In mid-1945, as the focus of World War II was moving from Europe to the Pacific, the American Office of Strategic Services (OSS) learned of a group of freedom fighters waging war against the Japanese in the French colony of Vietnam. The Viet Minh, led by revolutionary Ho Chi Minh, sought Vietnamese independence from foreign rule; when Japan occupied their country after France's defeat by the Nazis, the Viet Minh took up arms against them. Because of their common goal of Japanese defeat, in mid-July 1945, the American OSS sent a group of seven paratroopers into the Vietnamese jungle to train the Viet Minh in stealth combat and recovery techniques. The Americans delivered demolition equipment, automatic weapons, and even medical care—when the OSS arrived, the 55-year-old Ho Chi Minh was deathly ill. One of the OSS team, Paul Hoagland, was a nurse; he examined Ho, diagnosed him as suffering from severe dysentery and malaria, and treated him with quinine, sulfa drugs, and vitamins. Within ten days Ho was back on his feet. But the collaboration between the Americans and the Viet Minh lasted only until Japan surrendered on August 15, 1945. In the coming years, Ho Chi Minh sought to continue the alliance, writing several letters to President Truman asking for American support in the Vietnamese bid for independence from France, but his pleas for help went unanswered. Desperate for self-rule, Ho took assistance wherever he could find it, and by 1950 he'd discovered ready backers in Mao Zedong's Communist China and the Soviet Union. Eventually, the United States did enter Ho's war for independence, fighting against, rather than alongside, its old ally.

History Lesson: War makes strange bedfellows and enemies.

POL POT

Brother Number One, leader of the Khmer Rouge

BEST KNOWN FOR: Four-year dictatorship that led to death of 1.7 million Cambodians through starvation, overwork, disease, or execution • Forcing everyone—children, the elderly, hospital patients—into rural collectives to do agricultural work without aid of machinery • Abolishing money, markets, medical community, schools, and private property • Banning religion, holidays, music, entertainment, romance

BORN: May 19, 1925, as Saloth Sar, in Prek Sbauv

FAMILY: Eighth of nine children. Father was a land-owning farmer. Sent to live with brother, a clerk at the royal palace in Phnom Penh, when he was six. First wife hospitalized after nervous breakdown; married again in 1987 and had daughter with second wife.

EDUCATION: Failed high school entrance exams; studied carpentry at trade school instead. Received scholarship to study radio electronics in Paris, failed all examinations.

PHYSICAL DESCRIPTION: Elegant; delicate features, smooth face, agreeable smile, solid body, alert eyes. Feminine hands, dainty wrists.

FIRST JOB: Taught French, history, and civics at private school

LEAST KNOWN FOR: After the Vietnamese overthrew his government in 1979, Pol Pot denounced Communism for democracy; his government represented Cambodia in the United Nations until 1991

QUOTE: "I came to carry out the struggle, not to kill people. Even now, and you can look at me, am I a savage person?"

DEATH: April 15, 1998. On the day of his death, Pol Pot heard a Voice of America report that his former colleagues were turning him over to the Americans for trial; he lay down in his bed, and by 10 P.M. he was dead, either from heart failure or suicide.

HOW TO
PASSIVELY RESIST

⭐ Sign in when you arrive at a demonstration.
Organizers keep track of everyone at an event so they
are aware of who has been arrested or injured.

⭐ Always stay in pairs.
Never arrive at or leave an action alone.

⭐ Dress appropriately.
For marches or sit-ins where police may be present and
disruptive, men should wear clip-on ties so they cannot
be strangled by them. Women should wear comfortable
shoes, rather than high heels, to marches to allow for a
faster getaway. Neither men nor women should wear
any jewelry that can be yanked or pulled.

⭐ Prepare to be arrested.
Leave your car keys and personal items with someone
who is not planning to go to jail. Carry a toothbrush,
cigarettes (even if you don't smoke—they are useful cur-
rency with other inmates), and at least enough cash for
a phone call, if not more.

⭐ Make eye contact with the police.
To defuse anger, look officers in the eyes and show
them that you realize they are human and are doing
their job. Make them realize the same about you. Keep
your gaze compassionate or neutral; do not scowl or
furrow your brow.

Do not actively resist.

★ Sing.
Group singing creates strength and unity, helps to calm anxiety caused by the potential for violence and arrests, and provides an outlet for frustration. Songs also communicate your message and set a rhythm to the march or picket line. Encourage every participant to join in the singing, whether they feel they have a good voice or not—these songs are for protest and bonding as a group, not for showing off vocal talent.

★ Ignore teasing and taunting.
Do not react—vocally or physically—to jeers and name calling. The only appropriate response is to join the group in singing if the leader starts a song.

★ If you are arrested, go limp.
Fall to your knees and force the police to carry you to the bus or paddy wagon, but do not actively resist arrest. Call out your own name from the bus if you don't know if others saw that you were arrested. When you are interrogated, identify yourself to the police, but do not answer questions, and do not engage even friendly officers in conversation.

★ If the police attack, assume the nonviolent position.
If the police use force and you are not willing or unable to run from them, assume a nonviolent position: Put your head between your knees, with your elbows together in front of your eyes and your hands over your head to protect your skull. Try to shuffle close to a wall or a curb to protect your back. This position has a double benefit—it protects your vulnerable areas, and is

clearly nonthreatening to the police, eliciting sympathy from onlookers and the media.

Be Aware

A movement will have the most success if it is well organized and its followers are familiar with the plan. Hold training sessions so members of the group can participate in roleplaying skits to practice nonviolent reactions to stressful situations, learn protest songs, and plan for future actions.

HOW TO DEAL WITH TEAR GAS

1 Move upwind or crosswind of the gas.

2 Cover your mouth with your shirt or a piece of cloth.

3 Keep breathing.
Though your mouth, throat, and chest is burning, continue to try to breathe as normal. Your symptoms should clear up as soon as or shortly after you move away from the cloud of gas.

4 Remain standing.
Tear gas is a heavy vapor that settles close to the ground; crouching or kneeling will only increase your exposure.

5 Keep your hands away from your face and eyes.
Do not rub your eyes, as you will only irritate them more.

6 Wash away traces of the gas.

As soon as possible, flush out your eyes with water. Step out of your clothes; use scissors to cut off articles of clothing that must be pulled over your head. Wash your face and body with soap and water. Wash your clothes separately from the rest of your laundry, as they will contaminate other garments.

Be Aware

If you have reason to believe that the police will be using tear gas at an action, carry a moist handkerchief or wet towels with you and hold them over your mouth when the chemical is released.

WHO HAD IT WORSE?

	Richard Milhous Nixon	William Jefferson Clinton
Position	37th American president	42nd American president
Term	1969–1974	1992–2000
Party	Republican	Democrat
Challenges	Communists, anti-war protestors, Woodward and Bernstein	Vast right-wing conspiracy, Kenneth Starr
Deadly Sin	Pride	Lust
Bad Turning Point	Burglars found in Watergate building wiretapping the Democratic National Committee office	Linda Tripp records Monica Lewinsky admitting affair with Clinton, gives tapes to Special Prosecutor Kenneth Starr
Accusation	Nixon and aides illegally wiretapped Democratic competitors to maintain power	Clinton encouraged Lewinsky to lie about affair; committed perjury when testifying to Grand Jury
Statement	"I am not a crook."	"I did not have sexual relations with that woman."
Outcome	Resigned rather than face impeachment; pardoned by President Gerald Ford	Impeached, but acquitted by Senate; completed second term
Legacy	Opened U.S. relations with China	Presided over booming economy

IDI AMIN

His Excellency President for Life, Field Marshal Al Hadj Dr. Idi Amin Dada, VC, DSO, MC, Lord of All the Beasts of the Earth and Fishes of the Sea and Conqueror of the British Empire in Africa in General and Uganda in Particular

BEST KNOWN FOR: Executing 300,000 to 500,000 people, especially the Acholi and Langi ethnic groups, intellectuals, and anyone who spoke against him • Expelling 40,000 Ugandans of Asian origin • Establishing four competing secret police forces • Aiding Islamic terrorists who'd hijacked a plane full of Israeli citizens

BORN: c. 1925, Koboko, Uganda

FAMILY: Father, a farmer, separated from his mother soon after his birth; she took him to live in Nubian settlements. Had five wives and 32 children

PHYSICAL DESCRIPTION: 6'4", often dwarfed those in his presence. Wore a field marshal's uniform with an especially long tunic to display all the medals he awarded himself.

EDUCATION: Attended missionary school through sixth grade

FIRST JOB: Assistant cook in the King's African Rifles of the British colonial army; heavyweight boxing champion of Uganda, 1951–1960

NICKNAMES: Butcher of Uganda; Big Daddy

LEAST KNOWN FOR: Speaking six languages; declaring himself king of Scotland; banning hippies and mini skirts

QUOTE: "I myself consider myself the most powerful figure in the world."

DEATH: August 16, 2003, in exile in Saudi Arabia, of multiple organ failure after having been on life support for about a month

NUCLEAR POWER CATASTROPHE

On April 26, 1986, while scientists were conducting a test on reactor 4 of the Chernobyl Nuclear Power Station, a chain reaction took place in the reactor's core that quickly went out of control. The scientists, who had shut down the station's power regulating and emergency safety systems for the purpose of the experiment, reacted by making mistake after mistake. Within ninety minutes of the start of the test, the plant overheated, blasting the reactor's 1,000-ton steel-and-concrete lid through the roof and emitting a cloud of super-hot, radioactive steam and gas into the atmosphere. Wind blew the radioactive particles across the Ukraine and as far north as Norway, thousands of miles away. The USSR didn't acknowledge there had been a problem until officials at a reactor in Sweden noticed a giant upsurge in radioactivity in their area. The Soviets then released a vague statement: "An accident has taken place. . . . Measures are being taken to eliminate the consequences. . . . A government commission has been set up," without ever stating the simple, horrible truth: The open reactor was still burning, sending radiation into the outside world—and they had no idea how to stop it. Thirty-two people died in the incident, and although the reactor was contained by May 4, in the ensuing years thousands who lived near the plant developed cancer, and the frequency of birth defects is strikingly above normal. The full effects of the meltdown won't be known for years to come.

History Lesson: Admit your mistakes—quickly.

WORST HUMAN-CAUSED ENVIRONMENTAL ACCIDENTS

Event	Year	Description	Consequences
Soviet Nuclear Accident, Ural Mountains	1957	50 million curies of radiation released	Area the size of Rhode Island contaminated for 20 years
Torey Canyon Oil Spill, English Channel	1967	100,000 gallons crude oil released in water	Chemicals used in clean-up further poison water
Three Mile Island Nuclear Accident, Harrisburg, PA	1979	Malfunction causes overheating, near meltdown	Temporary closure of 7 other nuclear facilities, no new reactors ordered for U.S. until mid-'80s
Love Canal, Niagra Falls, NY	1955–1980	Chemical waste seeped into basements of homes built on former dumping ground	High rate of birth defects; evacuation of town, destruction of homes.
Gas Leak, Bhopal, India	1984	45-ton storage tank filled with insecticide leaks	Cloud of poison gas spreads over city, killing 2,000
Chernobyl Nuclear Disaster Prypyat, Ukraine, USSR	1986	Explosion, fire, 100 million curies of radio-nuclides released into atmosphere	Serious nuclear fallout in Belarus, Poland, and eastern Europe; radiation across northern Europe and UK
***Exxon Valdez* Oil Spill,** Prince William Sound, AK	1989	11 to 30 million gallons of crude oil released in water	Hundreds of thousands of animals killed
Toxic Waste, Guadimar River, Spain	1998	1.3 billion gallons of mining sludge released in river	25-mile stretch of river ruined; thousands of birds and fish killed

WORST OIL SPILL IN UNITED STATES HISTORY

On the night of March 23, 1989, the *Exxon Valdez* oil tanker was in the process of pulling through Prince William Sound when it changed course to avoid a group of small icebergs. But the tanker avoided the bergs only to rupture its hull on Bligh Reef, spilling 11 to 30 million gallons of crude oil into the water. The spill area eventually covered 11,000 square miles. Thousands of animals died as a result, including seals, orcas, sea otters, salmon, and hundreds of thousands of sea birds. The cleanup was thorough, but the spill had a lasting environmental impact—more than 15 years later many creatures continue to die because they eat contaminated animals, fish, or vegetation. The tanker's veteran captain, Joseph Hazelwood, was charged for intoxication at the scene of the accident, and though he did drink vodka that evening, he was cleared of crime. Exxon, meanwhile, was ordered to pay $5 billion in punitive damages and was still pursuing an appeal of the amount 17 years after the incident.

History Lesson: Oil and water don't mix.

HOW TO TREAT A BAD ACID TRIP

★ Remind the user that he is on acid.
The person who is tripping may think that he is dying or crazy. Use a calm, confident voice to reassure him that the negative thoughts and visions are just the effects of the drug and that they will wear off in time.

★ Suggest a timeframe for when the effects will wear off.
Sometimes people experiencing a bad trip feel like they are caught in eternity. Tell your friend that the effects of the drug will taper off within the next twelve hours.

★ Say his name.
Remind him of who he is; this may help to situate him back in the real world.

★ Ask him what negative thoughts he is having.
Tell the person to talk about what it is that he is experiencing so you can know where he is coming from.

★ Distract.
Change your friend's focus by talking about something innocuous, like a movie, a television show, or a recent pleasant experience you had together. Offer him a present he can hold and play with, like a small stuffed animal, a ring, a ball, a toy, something shiny, or a piece of string. Suggest that he take deep breaths, which will help him relieve some of the tension and negativity.

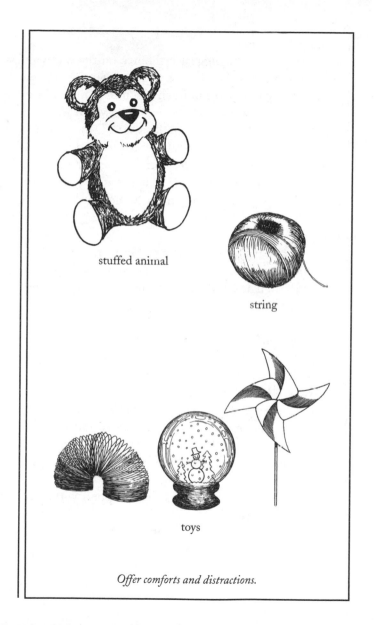

stuffed animal

string

toys

Offer comforts and distractions.

★ Change locations.
Environment is the biggest influence on the mind and emotions of the person who is tripping. Suggest to your friend that you get some fresh air, move into another room, or even over to the corner. Get away from flashing lights or stressful visual input. Other people, especially strangers, can escalate anxiety and paranoia, so take him out of a crowd or into a more private, quieter place. Do not force him to leave with you; gently coax him along if he is too afraid to move.

★ Listen to music.
Expose your friend to uplifting, happy, familiar music to help lighten the mood. You may suggest dancing to relieve tension and promote a more positive experience.

Be Aware

- If your friend is *seriously* freaking out, seek medical help. While a hospital experience will be unpleasant and may temporarily escalate your friend's panic and anxiety, if he is doing harm to himself or others it is the best alternative. The doctor will administer a sedative, likely chlorpromazine, to calm the effects of the LSD.
- Bad trips are more likely to occur if the user feels depressed, angry, anxious, or insecure before taking the acid.
- A person experiencing a bad trip may appear withdrawn, panicked, or scared.
- The effect of a dose of LSD intensifies over time, so be sure to stay with the person experiencing the bad trip.

RWANDAN GENOCIDE BEGINS WITH A PLANE CRASH

In April 1994, as Rwandan President Juvénal Habyarimana and Burundi President Cyprien Ntaryamira returned from peace talks between the Hutu and Tutsi ethnic groups, their plane was shot down and both men were killed. The violent death of the two Hutu leaders ignited full-scale genocide in Rwanda, where tribal tensions between Hutus and Tutsis had been smoldering for years. Hutus, blaming the Tutsis for the assassinations, formed death squads and began killing Tutsis at a horrifying rate. Using guns, hoes, machetes, and clubs, they slaughtered Tutsis by the thousands. In just 100 days, an estimated 800,000 Tutsis and moderate Hutus were murdered. The United Nations, which later revealed they'd been warned in advance of preparations for a genocide in Rwanda, did not intervene until after the worst of the bloodshed had taken place. The group responsible for bringing down the plane that sparked the violence has never been determined, though many now believe Hutu extremists to have been behind the attack.

History Lesson: It is easier to make war than peace.

SLOBODAN MILOSEVIC

President of Serbia; President of the Federal
Republic of Yugoslavia

BEST KNOWN FOR: Ethnic cleansing of Kosovar Albanians • Widespread killing and oppression of thousands of Bosnian Muslims and Bosnian Croats • Instigating the murder of hundreds of civilians and expelling 170,000 non-Serb Croats from their homes

BORN: August 29, 1941, in Pozarevac, the Republic of Serbia

FAMILY: Father left family when he was in grade school, committed suicide while he was at university. Raised by mother, a teacher and Communist activist, who hanged herself in 1974. Met wife, Mirjana "Mira" Markovic, in high school; had son, Marko, and daughter, Marija.

EDUCATION: Studied law at University of Belgrade

PHYSICAL DESCRIPTION: Somewhat rotund and baby-faced

FIRST JOBS: President of the state-owned gas company and, later, the president of the largest bank in Serbia

NICKNAMES: Slobo, The Butcher of the Balkans

LEAST KNOWN FOR: Acting as his own counsel during his war crimes trial at the Hague, submitting a list of 1,641 witnesses in his defense, including Bill Clinton and Tony Blair

QUOTE: "Serbia was not a warring party in Bosnia and Croatia. Serbia was trying to help the peace process to stop the fratricidal war."

DEATH: March 11, 2006, in his jail cell in the Hague. Though many supporters thought he was poisoned, and many detractors thought he committed suicide, formal autopsy confirmed that he died of heart failure.

OZONE LAYER HOLE IN 2000 VS. SIZE OF AFRICAN CONTINENT

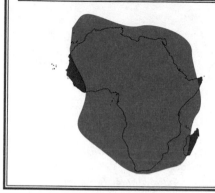

OZONE HOLE:
11.5 million square miles

AFRICAN CONTINENT:
11.7 million square miles

Y1K VS. Y2K

	Y1K	Y2K
Year	1000	2000
Fear	Last Judgment would be decreed in Jerusalem; world would end	The Y2K bug would cause technological meltdown
Action	Believers made pilgrimage to Jerusalem; many died in journey	Believers withdrew all money from banks, bought emergency supplies and rations, and hid in bunkers or other safehouses; companies spent $300 billion updating computer systems
Actual Result	Nothing happened	Minor security system problems in Japan; Australia reported trouble with bus-ticket validation machines; 150 slot machines malfunctioned at a Delaware racetrack
Aftermath	Returning pilgrims found homes ruined after years of neglect	Victims of paranoia pretended like they had never panicked

SELECTED SOURCES

BOOKS AND INTERVIEWS

Allcorn, William. *The Maginot Line 1928–45*. New York: Osprey Publishing, 2003.

Bartholomew-Feis, Dixee. *The OSS and Ho Chi Minh: Unexpected Allies in the War Against Japan*. Lawrence, Kansas: University Press of Kansas, 2006.

Bawden, Garth, and Richard Martin Reycraft, eds. *Environmental Disaster and the Archaeology of Human Response*. Albuquerque: Maxwell Museum of Anthropology, 2000.

Bedini, Silvio A. *The Pope's Elephant: An Elephant's Journey from Deep in India to the Heart of Rome*. New York: Penguin, 1997.

Bengtsen, Fiona. *Sir William Waad, Lieutenant of the Tower, and the Gunpowder Plot*. Oxford: Trafford Publishing, 2005.

Beyer, Rick. *The Greatest Stories Never Told*. New York: Harper Collins, 2003.

Blitzer, Charles, and the Editors of Time-Life Books. *Age of Kings*. New York: Time-Life Books, 1967.

Bodin, Lynn. *The Boxer Rebellion*. Oxford: Osprey Publishing, 1979.

Booth, Martin. *Opium: A History*. New York: St. Martin's Griffin, 1999.

Bown, Stephen R. *Scurvy: How a Surgeon, a Mariner, and a Gentleman Solved the Greatest Medical Mystery of the Age of Sail*. New York: St. Martin's Press, 2004.

Brackman, Roman. *The Secret File of Joseph Stalin: A Hidden Life*. London: Routledge, 2000.

Brands, H. W. *The Age of Gold: The California Gold Rush and the New American Dream*. New York: Doubleday, 2002.

Bryant, William Cullen. *A Popular History of the United States*. New York: C. Scribner's Sons, 1888.

Colton, Joel, and the Editors of Time-Life Books. *Twentieth Century*. New York: Time-Life Books, 1968.

Currey, Cecil B. *Victory at Any Cost: The Genius of Viet Nam's Gen. Vo Nguyen Giap*. Washington, DC: Potomac Books, 2005.

Dash, Mike. *Tulipomania*. New York: Three Rivers Press, 1999.

Davison, Michael Worth, ed. *Reader's Digest Everyday Life Through the Ages*. London: Reader's Digest Association, 1992.

de Madariaga, Isabel. *Ivan the Terrible: First Tsar of Russia.* New Haven, Connecticut: Yale University Press, 2005.

Department of the Army. *Combatives.* FM 3-25.150 (FM 21-150), January 18, 2002.

Dray, Philip. *Stealing God's Thunder: Benjamin Franklin's Lightning Rod and the Invention of America.* New York: Random House, 2005.

Duiker, William J. *Ho Chi Minh: A Life.* New York: Hyperion, 2000.

Dunbabin, Jean. *Captivity and Imprisonment in Medieval Europe, c. 1000–c. 1300.* New York: Palgrave Macmillan, 2003.

Elson, Henry William. *History of the United States of America.* New York: Macmillan, 1904.

Famous Adventures and Prison Escapes of the Civil War. New York: The Century Company, 1893.

Fawcett, Bill, and Brian Thomsen, eds. *You Did What? Mad Plans and Great Historical Disasters.* New York: Perennial Currents, 2004.

Fawcett, Bill, and William R. Forstchen, eds. *It Seemed Like a Good Idea . . . A Compendium of Great Historical Fiascoes.* New York: Quill, 2000.

Flexner, Stuart and Doris. *The Pessimist's Guide to History.* New York: HarperCollins, 1992, 2000.

Garrison, Webb. *Civil War Trivia and Fact Book: Unusual and Often Overlooked Facts About America's Civil War.* Nashville, Tennessee: Rutledge Hill Press, 1992.

Gay, Peter, and the Editors of Time-Life Books. *Age of Enlightenment.* New York: Time-Life Books, 1966.

Gillon, Steven M. *10 Days that Unexpectedly Changed America.* New York: Three Rivers Press, 2006.

Gombrich, E. H. *A Little History of the World.* Caroline Mustill, trans. New Haven, Connecticut: Yale University Press, 2005.

Gore, Al. *An Inconvenient Truth.* Emmaus, Pennsylvania: Rodale, 2006.

Harsin, Jill. *Barricades: The War of the Streets in Revolutionary Paris, 1830–1848.* New York: Palgrave Macmillan, 2002.

Hattikudur, Mangesh, Elizabeth Hunt, and Will Pearson, eds. *Mental_Floss Presents: Condensed Knowledge.* New York: HarperCollins, 2004.

———. *Mental_Floss Presents: Forbidden Knowledge.* New York: HarperCollins, 2005.

Heinemann, Evelyn. *Witches: A Psychoanalytic Exploration of the Killing of Women.* Donald Kiraly, trans. London: Free Association Books, 2000.

Peter Ifland is a commander in the U.S. Naval Reserve and author of *Taking the Stars: Celestial Navigation from Argonauts to Astronauts.*

Israel, Jonathan. *The Dutch Republic: Its Rise, Greatness, and Fall 1477–1806.* New York: Oxford University Press, 1998.

Johnson, Charles. *A General History of the Robberies and Murders of the Most Notorious Pyrates.* 1724.

Kenyon, Sherrilyn. *The Writer's Guide to Everyday Life in the Middle Ages.* Cincinnati, Ohio: Writer's Digest Books, 1995.

King, Ross. *Michelangelo and the Pope's Ceiling.* New York: Penguin Books, 2003.

Krupskaya, N. K. *Reminiscences of Lenin.* Bernard Issacs, trans. www.marxists.org/archive/krupskaya/works/rol/index.htm.

Benerson Little is a former Navy SEAL and special operations analyst. He is the author of *The Sea Rover's Practice: Pirate Tactics and Techniques, 1630–1730.*

Loftie, W. J. *Authorised Guide to the Tower of London.* London: Harrison and Sons, 1907.

Macgregor, Mary. *The Netherlands.* London: T. C. & E. C. Jack., 1907.

Man, John. *Gutenberg: How One Man Remade the World with Words.* New York: John Wiley & Sons, 2002.

Martin, James Kirby. *Benedict Arnold: Revolutionary Hero.* New York: New York University Press, 1997.

McCullough, David. *1776.* New York: Simon & Schuster, 2005.

Meyer, G. J. *A World Undone: The Story of the Great War 1914 to 1918.* New York: Delacorte Press, 2006.

Milton, Giles. *Nathaniel's Nutmeg: Or, the True and Incredible Adventures of the Spice Trader Who Changed the Course of History.* New York: Farrar, Straus and Giroux, 1999.

Monardes, Nicholas. *Joyfull Newes Out of the Newe Founde Worlde, 1577.* John Frampton, trans.; updated by Michael L. Wolfe, 1996. www.tobacco.org/History/monardes.html.

Morris, John. *The Life of Father John Gerard, of the Society of Jesus.* London: Burns and Oates, 1881.

Mourt's Relation: A Journal of the Pilgrims at Plymouth, 1622, Part I. Based on the Michigan University facsimile edition, updated by Caleb Johnson.

Robert Munman is a professor of art history at the University of Illinois at Chicago.

O'Brien, Cormac. *Secret Lives of the U.S. Presidents.* Philadelphia: Quirk Books, 2004.

Pavord, Anna. *The Tulip.* New York: Bloomsbury, 1999.

Pearson, Michael. *The Sealed Train.* New York: Putnam, 1975.

Pile, Stephen. *The Incomplete Book of Failures.* New York: E. P. Dutton, 1979.

Post, Dr. Jerrold M. and Robert S. Robins. *When Illness Strikes the Leader.* New Haven, Connecticut: Yale University Press, 1995.

Price, Munro. *The Road from Versailles: Louis XVI, Marie Antoinette, and the Fall of the French Monarchy.* New York: St. Martin's Press, 2003.

Rohrbough, Malcolm J. *Days of Gold: The California Gold Rush and the American Nation.* Berkeley, California: University of California Press, 1997.

Runciman, Steven. *The Fall of Constantinople 1453.* New York: Cambridge University Press, 1990.

Scott, Walter. *Life of Napoleon Bonaparte.* A & C Black, 1876.

Smith, William. *Dictionary of Greek and Roman Antiquities.* 1870. (www.ancientlibrary.com/smith-bio/index.html)

Spate, O.H.K. *The Spanish Lake: The Pacific Since Magellan, Volume I.* (http://epress.anu.edu.au/spanish_lake)

Stephens, John Richard. *Weird History 101.* Avon, Massachusetts: Adams Media Corporation, 1997.

Strachey, William. *The Historie of Travell into Virginia Britania. 1612.* Ed. Louis B. Wright and Virginia Freund. London: Printed for the Hakluyt Society, 1953.

Elizabeth Sweet studies at the University of Bristol, where she is performing a biochemical analysis of the saber-toothed cat.

Toland, John. *Adolf Hitler: The Definitive Biography.* New York: Anchor, 1991.

Wilson, Barry K. *Benedict Arnold: A Traitor in Our Midst.* Ithaca, New York: McGill-Queen's University Press, 2001.

Wiseman, John "Lofty." *The SAS Survival Handbook: How to Survive in the Wild, in Any Climate, on Land or at Sea.* London: HarperCollins Publishers, 1999.

Zacks, Richard. *An Underground Education.* New York: Anchor Books, 1997.

Zebrowski, Ernest. *The Last Days of St. Pierre: The Volcanic Disaster that Claimed 30,000 Lives.* New Brunswick, New Jersey: Rutgers University Press, 2002.

ARTICLES

Askwith, Richard, "How Aspirin Turned Hero," *Sunday Times* (South Africa), 13 September 1998.

"As Morphine Turns 200, Drug That Blocks Its Side Effects Reveals New Secrets." University of Chicago Medical Center, 19 May 2005.

Brooks, C. J. "Survival in Cold Waters." Marine Safety, Transport Canada. 24 August 2001.

Cadwallader, Lee C., and J. Stephen Herring. "Safety Issues with Hydrogen as a Vehicle Fuel." Idaho Falls: Idaho National Engineering and Environmental Laboratory, 1999.

Coleman, K. M. "Fatal Carades-Roman Executions staged as Mythological Enactments." *The Journal of Roman Studies,* 1990.

"Dance Marathons of the 1920s and 1930s—A Snapshot History." HistoryLink.org: The Online Encyclopedia of Washington State History. www.historylink.org/essays/output.cfm?file_id=5534

Edwards, John, and Al Seckel, "Franklin's Unholy Lightning Rod." *ESD Journal,* 2002.
http://esdjournla.com/articles/franklin/franklinrod.htm

Etkin, David. "Reducing Risk through Partnerships." Winnipeg, Manitoba: Canadian Risk Hazards Network, June 2005.

Fournie, Daniel A. "Hannibal's Epic March Across the Alps to Rome's Gates." *Military History,* March/April 2005.

Hartford, Bruce. "Notes from a Non-Violent Training Session (1963)." www.crmvet.org/info/nv1.htm

Hibbs, Peter A. "A.R.P. Fire Equipment."
www.nbcd.org.uk/arp/equipment/fire.asp

Howe, Mary Blye. "Safety First, at Last." *Invention & Technology Magazine,* Summer 1992.

"Infantry Tactics and Combat During the Napoleonic Wars."
http://web2.airmail.net/napoleon/infantry_tactics_3.htm

Kekes, John. "Why Robespierre Chose Terror." *City Journal*, April 19, 2006.

Korfmann, Manfred. "Was There a Trojan War?" *Archeology,* May/June 2004.

Luccketti, Nicholas M., William M. Kelso, and Beverly A. Straube. "Field Report 1994." APVA Jamestown Rediscovery, May 1994.

Malcolm, Corey. "The Mariner's Astrolabe." *The Navigator: Newsletter of The Mel Fisher Maritime Heritage Society,* May 1998.

Mayell, Hillary. "Climate Change Caused Extinction of Big Ice Age Mammals, Scientist Says." *National Geographic News*, 12 November 2001.

———. "Humans to Blame for Ice Age Extinctions, Study Says." National Geographic News, 10 August 2005.

Mellinkoff, Sherman M. "James Lind's Legacy to Clinical Medicine." *WJM*, April 1995.

Mitchell, Cerena V. "The Weathering of the Armada." *ICE Case Studies*, August 2005.

"Navigation Methods." Newfoundland and Labrador Heritage, 1997. www.heritage.nf.ca/exploration/navigate.html

Norris, Robert S., and Hans M. Kristensen. "Global Nuclear Stockpiles, 1945–2006." *Bulletin of the Atomic Scientists*, July/August 2006.

O'Leary, Captain Michael M. "A la Bayonet, or, 'Hot Blood and Cold Steel.'" *Journal of Non-lethal Combatives*, November 2000.

Paschall, Rod. "Paul Revere's True Account of the Midnight Ride." *MHQ: The Quarterly Journal of Military History*, Summer 2003.

Peterson, R. K. D. "Insects, Disease, and Military History: The Napoleonic Campaigns and historical Perception." *American Entomologist*, 41.

"Protection in the Nuclear Age." Federal Emergency Management Agency, June 1985.

Revere, Paul. "Letter to Jeremy Belknap." 1798. Manuscript Collection, Massachusetts Historical Society.

Searles, Priscilla. "Benedict Arnold, Business Man." *Business New Haven*, May 1, 1994.

Stillman, Anne. "Fences and the Settlement of New England." *Blueprints*, Summer 1996.

Wert, Jeffry D. "George Armstrong Custer: Between Myth and Reality." *Civil War Times*, March/April 2006.

Wright, Karen. "Empires in the Dust." *Discover Magazine*, March 1998.

WEBSITES

Academy of Saint Gabriel (www.s-gabriel.org)

Africans in America (www.pbs.org/wgbh/aia/home.html)

Albert Einstein's Letters to President Franklin Delano Roosevelt (hypertextbook.com/eworld/einstein.shtml)

"America and the Holocaust," *American Experience*
   (www.pbs.org/wgbh/amex/holocaust)
americancivilwar.com
American Social History Productions (historymatters.gmu.edu)
The Armoury Online (thearmouryonline.co.uk)
Asia for Educators, Columbia University
   (afe.easia.columbia.edu)
astrolabes.org
bbc.co.uk/history
The Canadian Encyclopedia (www.thecanadianencyclopedia.com)
civilwarhome.com
Civvy Street in World War 2 (www.macksites.com/PRT1.htm)
Colonial House (www.pbs.org/wnet/colonialhouse)
Crime Library, Court TV (www.crimelibrary.com)
"Dead Men's Tales," *Scientific American Frontiers*
   (www.pbs.org/saf/1203/index.html)
Decameron Web
   (www.brown.edu/Departments/Italian_Studies/dweb)
"Dot.Con," *Frontline* (www.pbs.org/wgbh/pages/frontline/shows/
   dotcon)
Encyclopedia Titanica (www.encyclopedia-titanica.org)
englishmonarchs.co.uk
"Escape!" *Nova* (www.pbs.org/wgbh/nova/escape)
eyewitnesstohistory.com
The First World War (www.firstworldwar.com)
The Gold Rush (www.pbs.org/goldrush)
The Good Drugs Guide (www.thegooddrugsguide.com)
historicroyalpalaces.org
historybuff.com
Illustrated History of the Roman Empire (www.roman-empire.net)
In Search of Shakespeare (www.pbs.org/shakespeare)
Internet History Sourcebooks Project (www.fordham.edu/halsall)
Internet Modern History Sourcebook, Fordham University
   (www.fordham.edu/halsall/mod/modsbook.html)
KI4U, Inc. (www.ki4u.com)
Legendary Lighthouses (www.pbs.org/legendarylighthouses/index.html)
Livius: Articles on Ancient History (www.livius.org)
"Lost at Sea: The Search for Longitude." *Nova*
   (www.pbs.org/wgbh/nova/longitude)

luther.de/en/index.html

Martin Luther (www.pbs.org/empires/martinluther)

mayflowerhistory.com

Medici: Godfathers of the Renaissance (www.pbs.org/empires/medici)

Military History Online (www.militaryhistoryonline.com)

Mortal Women of the Trojan Wars (www.stanford.edu/~plomio/history.html)

nationalgeographic.com

"Nazi Prison Escape," *Nova* (www.pbs.org/wgbh/nova/naziprison/escapes.html)

nefertiti.iwebland.com

New Perspectives on the West (www.pbs.org/weta/thewest)

"Patriots Day," *American Experience* (www.pbs.org/wgbh/amex/patriotsday)

Perseus Digital Library (www.perseus.tufts.edu)

pitwork.net

The Plymouth Colony Archive Project (etext.virginia.edu/users/deetz/Plymouth)

"Race for the Superbomb," *American Experience* (www.pbs.org/wgbh/amex/bomb)

Red Files (www.pbs.org/redfiles/)

Red Gold: The Epic Story of Blood (www.pbs.org/wnet/redgold)

"Roots of a War (1945–1953)," *Vietnam: A Television History; American Experience* (www.pbs.org/wgbh/amex/vietnam)

sailtexas.com

"Search for the First Human," *Secrets of the Dead* (www.pbs.org/wnet/secrets/case_firsthuman/index.html)

"Secrets of Lost Empires: Medieval Siege," *Nova* (www.pbs.org/wgbh/nova/lostempires/trebuchet)

"Surviving the Dustbowl," *American Experience* (www.pbs.org/wgbh/amex/dustbowl)

Titanic Historical Society, Inc. (www.titanic1.org)

touregypt.net

"The Triumph of Evil," *Frontline* (www.pbs.org/wgbh/amex/bomb)

The Victorian Web (www.victorianweb.org)

Virtual Museum of the City of San Francisco (www.sfmuseum.org)

Washington State University: World Civilizations (www.wsu.edu:8001/~dee)

The West (www.pbs.org/weta/thewest)

World War I Document Archive (www.gwpda.org)
World War II Online Museum
(www.worldwar2exraf.co.uk/Online%20Museum/
Museum%20Docs/Onlinemuseumhomepage.html)
The Worst Jobs in History
(www.channel4.com/history/microsites/W/worstjobs/index.html)
Xenophon Group (www.xenophongroup.com/xenogrp.htm)

Newspapers, Magazines, Other Publications, and Organizations

American Canoe Association
American Geological Institute
American Institute of Physics
American Museum of Natural History
Association for the Preservation of Virginia Antiquities
Australian Museums & Galleries Online
BBC
British Library
Center for History and New Media, George Mason University
Centers for Disease Control
Chicago Historical Society
Connecticut Society of the Sons of the American Revolution
Department of Mathematics and Computer Science, Philipps-
Universität, Germany
Department of the Navy, Naval Historical Center
Detroit News
Encyclopedia Americana
Encyclopedia Britannica
Eskind Biomedical Library, Special Collections Digital Library,
Vanderbilt Medical Center
Federal Bureau of Investigation
Guardian
The History Channel
Illinois State Museum
Independence Hall Association
Innovative Teaching Concepts
Institute of Human Origins, Arizona State University
International Union for Conservation of Nature and Natural
Resources

Johnson Space Center, National Aeronautics and Space
    Administration
Massachusetts Office of Coastal Zone Management
Medieval Crime Museum, Rothenburg, Germany
Metropolitan Museum of Art
Museum of Paleontology, University of California, Berkeley
National Coal Mining Museum for England
National Maritime Museum, Greenwich, England
National Oregon/California Trail Center, Monpelier, Idaho
National Park Service, U.S. Department of the Interior
New York Times
North Carolina Maritime Museum
Occupational Safety & Health Administration, U.S. Department of
    Labor
Old World Contacts, Applied History Research Group, University of
    Calgary
Ottawa Citizen
The Paul Revere Memorial Association
Pirate Soul Museum
Pitcairn Islands Study Center
"Revolution—1917." *The First World War: The Complete Series*, DVD,
    directed by Marcus Kiggell and Simon Rockell. Wark Clements,
    Hamilton Films Production: 2004.
Royal Observatory, Greenwich, England
San Francisco Chronicle
Schaffer Library of Drug Policy
Smithsonian
Stars and Stripes
Supreme Court Historical Society
Time
Time: Asia Edition
Toronto Star
U.S. Census Bureau
U.S. Department of State
U.S. Geological Survey, U.S. Department of the Interior
U.S. News & World Report
Washington Crossing Historic Park: Pennsylvania Historical and
    Museum Commission
Washington Post

INDEX

Acknowledgments

Josh Piven thanks his co-authors, editors, illustrators, designers, and the History Channel.

Oscar Wilde once wrote that "[A]ny fool can make history, but it takes a genius to write it," so Dave Borgenicht would like to thank all the geniuses and fools who can now truly say they have "made history." He'd like to thank his co-authors, in particular Melissa Wagner, without whom this book would certainly not have been possible and history would have stopped being recorded. He'd also like to thank Jay Schaefer, Steve Mockus, and Micaela Heekin for their insightful and creative development, writing, and whip-cracking throughout the making of this book. Finally, he'd like to thank Bob O'Mara for his terrific design and illustrations, Brenda Brown for her continually remarkable work, and Mike Rogalski for his stalwart design leadership, can-do attitude, and ability to laugh at adversity.

Piers Marchant wishes to thank his two excellent research assistants, Matt Gray and Reyna Howkins, for their tireless effort, and his wife, Audrey, for putting up with endless anecdotes about the Middle Ages.

Melissa Wagner would like to thank Jay, Steve, and Micaela for their forbearance and encouragement; Dave, Josh, and Piers for their great ideas; illustrator Brenda for making history come alive; designer Bob for his remarkable work, even as all of New Jersey flooded and everything stopped making sense; design director Mike for his constant good humor; Faatima Qureshi for her excellent research; editors Erin, Kevin, and Jason for picking up the slack while she lived in the past; and her family, friends, and co-workers for at least feigning interest in her new-found knowledge. Most of all, she would like to thank her husband, Chris Ballod, for his patience, support, caretaking, humoring, and self-sacrificing during the vacationless "worst-case summer" of 2006.

ABOUT THE AUTHORS

Joshua Piven didn't always understand history, so in high school he was condemned to repeat it. Now he knows that what's past is prologue. He is the co-author, with David Borgenicht, of the Worst-Case Scenario series. He and his family live in Philadelphia.

David Borgenicht is the publisher of Quirk Books (www.quirkbooks.com) and the co-author of all of the books in the Worst-Case Scenario series. He was a history major in college but has since been demoted to lieutenant. He lives in Philadelphia, very much in the present.

Piers Marchant is a writer living in Philadelphia with his wife and daughter. He has written books on various subjects, including *How to Be Pope*.

Melissa Wagner is an editor and writer who lives and works in Philadelphia.

Brenda Brown is an illustrator and cartoonist whose work has been published in many books and publications, including the Worst-Case Scenario series, *Esquire, Reader's Digest, USA Weekend, 21st Century Science & Technology*, the *Saturday Evening Post*, and the *National Enquirer*. Her website is http://webtoon.com.

THE FIRST OF THE WORST

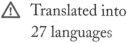 3 million copies in print

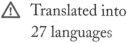 Translated into 27 languages

 International best-seller

"An armchair guide for the anxious."
—*USA Today*

"The book to have when the killer bees arrive."
—*The New Yorker*

"Nearly 180 pages of immediate action drills for when everything goes to hell in a handbasket."
—*Soldier of Fortune*

"This is a really nifty book."
—*Forbes*

A BOOK FOR EVERY DISASTER

⭐ *The Worst-Case Scenario Survival Handbook*

⭐ *The Worst-Case Scenario Survival Handbook: Travel*

⭐ *The Worst-Case Scenario Survival Handbook: Dating & Sex*

⭐ *The Worst-Case Scenario Survival Handbook: Golf*

⭐ *The Worst-Case Scenario Survival Handbook: Holidays*

⭐ *The Worst-Case Scenario Survival Handbook: Work*

⭐ *The Worst-Case Scenario Survival Handbook: College*

⭐ *The Worst-Case Scenario Survival Handbook: Weddings*

⭐ *The Worst-Case Scenario Survival Handbook: Parenting*

⭐ *The Worst-Case Scenario Book of Survival Questions*

⭐ *The Worst-Case Scenario Survival Handbook: Extreme Edition*

⭐ *The Worst-Case Scenario Survival Handbook: Life*

MORE WORST-CASE SCENARIOS FOR EVERY SEASON

→ The Worst-Case Scenario Survival Calendar
→ The Worst-Case Scenario Daily Survival Calendar
→ The Worst Case Scenario Daily Survival Calendar: Golf
→ The Worst-Case Scenario Dating & Sex Address Book
→ The Worst-Case Scenario Sticky Situation Notes

Watch for these WORST-CASE SCENARIO games at retailers near you or at: